T0065638

IN THE CIRCUIT COURT OF COOK COUNTY, ILLINOIS

THE PEOPLE OF THE STATE OF ILLINOIS

vs.

DESCRIPTION & LOCATION

1st Degree Murder

PHYSICAL EVIDENCE

LABORATORY UNIT

FIREARMS

NOT VALID FOR SERVICE ON NEWS MEDIA WITHOUT ORDER OF COURT

INCIDENT/OFFENSE CLASSIFICATION

HOMICIDE / MURDER

Fatal Gun Shot to Chest

(1) Lorcin mod L380 380 cal semi

CRIME SCENE PROCESSING REPORT
CHICAGO POLICE DEPARTMENT

CRIME LABORATORY REPORT
CRIME LABORATORY DIVISION/CHICAGO POLICE

EVIDENCE OF INJURY:

THAT I'M NOT, I'LL NEVER BE

The Diary, Cook County Jail Division 1 Chronicles

Appahummie the Author

ARCHWAY
PUBLISHING

This book is a work of non-fiction. Unless otherwise noted, the author and the publisher make no explicit guarantees as to the accuracy of the information contained in this book and in some cases, names of people and places have been altered to protect their privacy.

Archway Publishing books may be ordered through booksellers or by contacting:

Archway Publishing
1663 Liberty Drive
Bloomington, IN 47403
www.archwaypublishing.com
844-669-3957

ISBN: 978-1-6657-4087-6 (sc)
ISBN: 978-1-6657-4088-3 (e)

Library of Congress Control Number: 2023905228

Print information available on the last page.

Archway Publishing rev. date: 04/27/2023

Contents

"Special Thanks"

Off top, I would like to thank my Higher Power for keeping me safe and healthy, and also for giving me the strength and motivation to continue on my writing journey and never give up no matter how hard things get overtime, I thank you for keeping my family safe and healthy as well, I understand without you there's no me. You told me if I do my half you got me covered, I listened and believed and here we are.

Thank you, Mom, for unconditionally loving and never giving up on me, I love you, your first son.

Thank you, Granddad, for instilling in me the Morals, character, and teachings I still exercise to this day, I Love you Granddad.

To all my siblings, Thank you for always having my back right or wrong, and always loving me unconditionally no matter what.

Thank you, to all the significant people that played a positive role in my life

Rest In Peace to all the loved ones I've lost on this journey of life

Thank you, to the whole city of Chicago Illinois, where it all started.

Special Thanks, to my entire staff and a host of others that contributed on the way, thank you for everything and all the work you do.

To all my up-and-coming writers don't give up, weather the storm, the world needs your content so give them what they want.

Sincerely, Appahummie The Author.

The story you about to read has been fictionalized for dramatic purposes so some names, events, and characters has been changed and catered for the reader, but lets just say "if you know, you know".

I

Bloody Weekend Leaves Eight Dead

A blazing turbulent turmoiled Friday night, and Saturday morning, sources say, leave eight Chicagoans dead from shootings and several others wounded …

… A 20-year-old man was shot to death Friday night. Police identify him as Darius Brown, a resident of the southwest suburbs. Sources say he was sitting in a parked car around 9 pm Friday when he was approached by three men, one of whom yelled gang slogans and opened fire with a handgun. All three suspects were apprehended fleeing the scene and charged with first-degree murder Saturday evening, Chicago Tribune sources say.

II

These Men No Man
Should Call Friends

A Murderous Tale about the Notorious
Cook County Jail Division 1
The Darkside

October of 1994 is something I'll never forget, or shall I say, never want to remember. Damn this can't be real. Is this really happening to me? Shit feels like I'm dreaming, but I'm pretty much woke, having a nightmare with my eyes wide open, it seems. Cuffed and shackled, in a single-file line as we walk down this gloomy, dark, underground tunnel hallway to booking. Yeah, I can already see ain't no time for games because it's too much going on, from loud, overly aggressive dudes shaking up, gangbanging, and shit, to dope fiends nodding everywhere, plus this bitch jammed packed like the fourth of July.

"Listen up, listen up," officer yells. "At this time, whatever the fuck you got on you that don't suppose to be there, you better throw that shit on the line in front of you now, cause if we find it on your possession we gon' beat yo' motherfucking ass, simple as that. And you got another case, so test it, if you want." The officer's words damn near made the whole line start reaching for body parts, some hiding shit, and the rest throwing shit on the line. I ain't got nothing on me, nor am I testing anything, so I'm good. But damn, it sounds like a football game in this bitch, I can't even hear myself think from these loud-ass niggas. This is another world, and truth be told I'm practically scared to death about my circumstances. But ain't no pussy in me, so I'm standing on all ten, following rules and minding my business.

I wont be here long, so I'm good, but this gotta be the longest night ever..

"Step forward," the guard screams. I oblige. "Put your hand right here for fingerprints." I do the eye test, etc, and get changed out to a tan DOC fit. Single file line, we walk as niggas get dropped off to different decks en route. Division Five 2L, the school wing, is where my flesh landed.

"On the new. On the new," is what they screaming while running up to the door on some gangbanging shit, throwing up signs.

"What you is? What you is?" A small group of niggas saying while crowding the entrance as I walk through the door

"I'm Treys," I reply, tucking my pinky finger with my thumb, and throwing up three fingers in their face. "Now what you is?" I ask. He walks off silenced with disappointment, calling my kind for me.

The first dude heading my way, a lil big-head, cock-strong, tongue-tied nigga, with his T-shirt tied on his head. "Oh shit, what's up, BD?" my boy Pootie yells as he approaches.

"What's up, folks?" I replied. "So this where you been put up at."

"Yeah, bro, I been here for two years and ready to get the fuck away from these kids." We clench fists and walk off through the jam-packed dayroom, while everybody watches.

"Folks, where your hygiene and shit at?" he asks. All I can do is shrug my shoulders and keep walking because they ain't gave me nothing, nada, zero. Not a towel, toothbrush, soap, mattress, or anything else that new inmates get kitted with upon entry. So the guys grab me a mat, a few snacks, and some personal hygiene from the BD box.

At this time the deck jam-packed, with three men in a two-man cell. With no room in any of my guys' cells, my mat is laid outside of Pootie's door on the lower level. I put my lil shit up in his room and come out looking around, flabbergasted, watching niggas horseplaying, wrestling, throwing water and shit, like big-ass kids. Now I see and understand why they call this the school wing. A deck full of young black men with cases. I never considered my age is why I was sent here, but here I am.

I'm really locked the fuck up and need to make a phone call. But noticed one Lil light skinned 4Corner Hustler with short cornrows to the back just riding the phone, with security by his side. They basically took over that phone from what I'm seeing. And it's only one more for fifty or more inmates, but bullshit, another guy wanna use that exact phone. And from the look of things, he's getting angrier by the second. "When he hangs up, he better get up," he says while watching him like a hawk. Mean mugs and cold stares from both parties—something's about to happen, my intuition alerts me—and *boom*—he swing on his security, and the whole damn room just goes into an uproar.

What the fuck? as I instantly hop the rail to the lower level for safety, thinking to myself, *Not this on my first day in here.* But I'm composed, with my back to the wall and guards up, ain't nobody gunning for me. So I'm good. They getting it in though, a room full of young, energetic dudes screaming, punching, stabbing, and throwing shit barbaric style, a free-fall is what we call it.

Shortly after the guards flood the unit, smacking mafuckas up (lock up, lock up) while yanking a few in the hallway. In the midst of the chaos, they end up putting me in an empty two-man cell. I'm the first in the room, sitting on the lower bunk, when the door pops, and three men enter. "Ay, bro, you gotta get up. That's my bed."

"This our room," one of the men says. I get up humbly with no questions asked. "What you is?" are his next words.

"BD," I reply with the clenched fist and my chest out.

"We Blackstone take the neutron mat," he says as if he's not even standing here. I don't pray on the weak.

"I'm cool till these doors pop," I reply. Then I sit and lay in my little corner for a few hours.

"Dotts," the intercom blares, knocking me out a slight nod. The door pops, and just that quick, I am on my way to where all the alleged killers hang out. *Division I, damn.* This is where you *die* if you weak. Hell, even the strong don't make it here, and I'm thrown in this bitch blindly, here we fucking go.

III

Stay Strong from a Boy to a Man

I can't believe this shit. Here I am, barely an eighteen-year-old kid in the flesh, ready to adjust on the fly in the belly of the beast with grown seasoned criminals. Most with not shit to lose, at all. I weigh about one-thirty soaking wet, fully dressed in my boots, but I'm smart and know how to protect myself. But most of all, I definitely mind my business, for sure.

Cook County Jail 1994, ain't about fighting cases; it's about something way more sinister. The look in these grown men's eyes as I three-sixty my surroundings, confirms what the fuck I done got myself into. I'm nervous but composed and definitely standing on my shit amongst alleged killers, robbers, rapists, drug dealers, and all different walks of life, which you couldn't imagine. "Single file line. Single file line!" the officer screams. "Shut the fuck up and pay attention to the words that's coming out my mouth." My antenna's straight up in the air because this is unfamiliar territory for me. So I'm all eyes, ears, and no mouth.

The route to Division 1 is like no other, guided down a long, dark, scary tunneled hallway area, known as the "Boulevard," which leads to my temporary housing for now. The feeling of being a hostage starts to overwhelm me for a brief moment while walking to the B-Whale. "Dotts, this yo' stop (B2) second floor," the guard says and chuckles; "be safe." Reader, listen up, a quick intel on Division1 housing setup. A-Whale through the G-Whale. Each Whale houses four different decks containing forty-five inmates per floor.

Introducing inmate 9462414—welcome to hell.

The first sight of this deck fuck me straight up, I can't lie. All bars, no privacy. I see everything, and everything sees me. Face-to-face with a deck full of alleged killers, some scrambling and climbing the bars, screaming, "On the new. On the new. What you is?"

"What the fuck? I'm BD. What y'all is?" I scorn back sarcastically. I'm looking around in total amazement like I'm at the fucking zoo. If I was built different, I'd be spooked right now, but the unconvincing scare tactics they displaying can't and won't budge me.

(Nacho, Cheese)

The quarter gate pops, and I walk in with only a rolled-up mat and an eighty-mile-an-hour heartbeat. (*BD, BD.*) Several cats are already screaming to the back to alert the Nation I'm here, and out the back pops a few BDs with one familiar face I know. June Bug, aka JB, from the hood, my man. Quick intel: June Bug is one of the hot-head guys, but cool as a fan if ain't shit going on. Allegedly, I repeat, allegedly he is in for getting down on two of the GDs about some paper he owed, eighty thousand or so, and they need that.

*

"Ring, Ring," hello. "Where you at, where you at?" a voice blares through his brick phone as soon as he answers. ("JB, we on our way to you," the driver says.)

Pull up: "You know where I'm at," JB replies. (There he goes walking, catch up and pull over.) "What's up, Joe?"

"Get in," the passenger states while looking around,unsure. JB hops in behind the passenger eating a big bag of Cheese Doritos.

"Give me a few of them chips," the driver asks.

"It's over, they gone," JB responds, leaning back, licking his fingers, as the butter-soft leather seats melt under his oversized Girbaud shorts.

"You got that we kind of in a rush," driver says.

"Yeah, yeah. Go straight and bust a left and pull over. Right here. Yeah, right here, and cut yo' lights out."

"It's dark as hell back here, hurry up," the passenger blurts out as they park.

"How you in the streets, but scared of the dark, nigga?" JB responds, while easing his hand to the door handle.

Pow, pow as fire blows through the chip bag, into the back of the debt collectors' skulls, slumping them both. The shots light up the dark like the Fourth of July, and just that fast JB's gone before the smoke clears, disappearing into the night through the hood, unnoticed.

Boom boom boom. "This JB, open up, open up."

"Who the fuck is it, who is it," Mookie yells while yanking open the door. "Man, what the fuck, JB? Come on. What you then did? What happen, Folks?"

"What you mean?" JB replies.

"You got blood and—what the fuck is this, crunched-up Doritos or some shit all over your fucking jacket and your chin, that's what I mean."

"I know I know I know" JB drenches his face with cold kitchen sink water. Uneasy about the situation, and still gasping for air, with a dripping beard he blurts out, "I just had to stretch two mafuckas and get outta there."

"Damn, Folks, why you come here? You gon' have my shit on fire," he replied. "Here, JB, take this jacket and bounce."

"Gimme a second, Mook, damn, gimme a second," as he mean-mugs, putting on the oversized jacket.

"Hurry up and bounce, JB. You got my number; just page me."

"Ok, I'm gone and good-looking," JB replies, jetting out the door.

No sooner than he exits the premises, Mookie calls the police, telling what he knows and giving up the oversized jacket description that he so-called blessed JB with. What a bitch 'that dude is, because I personally know him as well, but this is just how this street shit goes. Needless to say, he probably owed the law a favor, or some niggas just born bitch like that. Either way, stay woke.

*

That just an insight on JB's alleged situation, anyway. "What up Joe? What you in here for?" he asks, greeting and saluting me, with an excited tone and the happiest expression on his mug.

"A 9-1, murder," I reply, feeling more fucked up every time I speak it in the air. "Damn, this where you been. I ain't seen you in a minute, JB."

"Hell yea, I been MIA. This shit fucked up, but come on, I'm about to put dude out my cell real quick."

Mean mugs and cold stares from grown men is the only thing I see in my peripheral as we breeze through the dayroom to the back. "Ay, Joe, pack yo' shit. My lil cuz right here," JB states to his celly. The dude instantly hops up, grabs his mat and other lil shit, and hauls ass out the door, no questions asked.

A few of the guys from 45th, 100z, and some other spots pull up on me at the cell. "You know some pieces?" one of the guys asks me.

"Yeah," I reply and spit something, plus JB vouching for me a hundred, so it's good. They also feel the need to ask if I know anything about the lil Yummy situation since I'm from the hundreds as well. "No," I answer, but I definitely heard about that bullshit right before I landed here.

After all the questions and screening, they hit me with a little care package out of the BD box: a shank, a couple of hygiene products, snacks, etc. We then speak about security purposes for a hot second, before they disappear.

"What's been going on with you and family BD?" a frantic JB asks.

"Everybody okay," I answer, and we reminisce about the hood in every way possible. I make him feel like he's out there with us. He also asks about his girlfriend, despite her being in the block every day, all day, with one of the older folks, but I say I never see her.

As we talk on, all of a sudden he gets quiet, staring at the ceiling. "These bitches gave me natural life plus fifty years." His voice crackles as he exhales.

Damn, bro, that's fucked up, I think but don't say a word, while shaking my head in sorrow. After he regroups himself, 50 Cent and Nate Dogg ain't got shit on him, 'cause he starts back asking twenty-one questions.

This, man can't shut up, so I keep talking all night long to take his mind away for a minute, till we fade out. Can you imagine his mental state after fighting murder and attempt for years? I can't, but I do understand he is tired, and just waiting to be shipped off to prison.

Niggas ain't fucking around in here at all. Everyone doing what they feel right for their situation at this moment. All of us want out of this county jail, so both genders copping out, like forty going north. Let's not forget, a lot of niggas taking time to avoid getting killed in this bitch as well. So with all this gumbo of shit stewing together, everything, I mean everything Clenched Fist) in this bitch with me and mine; ain't shit personal.

The loud popping of the doors awakes us, springing me up like a fireman on call early dew hours, for breakfast. I ain't brushed not a tooth in my mouth, but I'm out the door hungry as a hostage, ready and willing to bang whatever they bring through that gate. *This should be interesting,* I think, gazing the room from our table, as niggas grab trays out of the interlock for their mobs. I instantly pray over my food and start smashing the Akunu slop ASAP. With a mouth full of slop, I listen in silence as the guys gossip about another nigga, like he Al Capone or some shit. I really wanna tell them to shut the fuck up, dick-riding one of the guys named Tory, who allegedly run the jail for the BDs. I mean they talking about this nigga like he nine feet tall. Tory flying kites all around this bitch, like he at the beach or something searching for CM to blast him for whatever reason. I know neither of them nor anybody else to give a fuck about their shit right now. It's foolish if you ask me because my attention solely focused on my surroundings and how I'ma get the fuck up outta here—nothing more, nothing less.

As they gossip away, I three-sixty the dayroom with one swift glance, clearly visualizing horrible scenarios in my head. So this is where forty-five inmates gotta live, day in and day out, with all different personalities, attitudes, and whatever else comes with niggas in jail. Sooner or later shit is bound to go up with violence at some point, I'm knowing.

The devil's playground is exactly what this place is. Just the nastiness alone makes every day in this bitch extra stressful and miserable, not to mention rats running everywhere forcing us to grease our bars and hang our bags of commissary at the top, so our shit don't get ate up.

Although I can't show a pinch of how I'm really feeling, it oozes through men and their actions, and such behavior always keeps us on red alert. You either follow these jail rules that's been laid down in here forever, or die. Yeah, I said it: die, that's just how shit goes around here, no love. I understood what I was up against in the free world, but this here is a whole other level of chaos to the third power.

As the sun and the moon chase each other, our lives are pretty much on repeat, with the same routine: shit, shower, and shave; learn faces and the skills I need to survive in the jungle. Learning my oppositions is the easy part 'cause if you ain't with us, you against us. My character and how I move around this bitch, keep niggas guessing what's on my mental. With that combined behavior, I became a nigga that all the alleged killers pay close attention to.

Instantly the streets are off my mind, cause shit going on around me that requires my undivided attention as well. These decks going up, due to chain reactions and alleged killers getting banked all around Division 1 like pinball machines.

IV

(A Strong Presence)
(Why Me?)

"On the new, on the new," *clack, clack*—the gate pops, and out of the blue enters a six-foot slender, brown-skinned, circle-faced dude with a half head of connected braids to the back. This man walks in eating a chocolate Nemo cake like it's his birthday or some shit. I'm watching him from afar and notice a shifty, shysty look about himself. Personally, I think nothing of it, or him, at first sight, but the guys confirm he's the CM for the mob amongst our greet and salute. You know, they say, you can never judge a book by its cover, and that's real shit. *So this the nigga they keep talking about blasting*, I'm thinking to myself. He is a guest in the building, meaning he the number one man, Tory, who runs the jail number two as long as they under the same roof, sort of like a landlord and tenant.

Although Tory runs the jail, CM power gives him the authority to override anything that's going on, all while following the same laws and policies as everyone else. However,

CM informed us that he was banked over here, because some shit happen in Division 9 and he wasn't fucking with the GDs and the One Love concept that's been laid down to be honored at this time. He also mentioned Tory got him violated for it, and this is still Tory's jail, despite the punishment he received off Tory's command. I don't care not one grain about that shit, but I'm constantly hearing Tory's name like he the big bad wolf around this bitch, huffing and puffing.

As the days and nights slowly move on, me and CM start rotating with each other a lil more than the rest of the guys. We clique and become everyday Black Devil Disiples. I kid you not, I begin to learn this nigga, as well as his moves and his mindset, and come to the conclusion, this man a fucking lunatic in real life, to say the least. I promise you, big on power and running shit over as he goes.

Check it out, Big BD: CM calls the security outside the door. "What's up?"

"Go grab me a chocolate Nemo out the box, and tell him to put my name down for it."

"Okay," Big BD responds and disappears, leaving us back to our game of casino. I'm sitting here tripping cause he be geeking for them damn cakes like it's crack in it.

"Man, watch the board." (I am.)

Four and up, seven, ten. "Damn, you got the king of diamond. That's game."

"I know." CM shysty smirks as if he cheated.

Tap, tap. "Bless this house," Big BD says and enters empty-handed. He says, "Ain't no more cakes.

CM springs to his feet like a gymnast. "What he mean ain't no more cakes? Niggas just went to commissary two days ago."

"I don't know," Big BD replies, shrugging.

"Matter of fact, go get that box sheet and bring it here." Big BD takes off yet again, and I can already see where this is heading. "Whoever got that box better hope they shit in order," CM blurts out, still pissed over ain't no more Chocolate Nemo cakes.

"Bless this house." Big BD reenters with paper in hand.

CM instantly scowls at the paper and starts shaking his head in sorrow. "Do you mean to tell me this motherfucker ate four cakes and only two for one the other two? Big BD, call the back," CM suggests, "and tell folks who run the box to be front and center."

"BD's got the back, BD's got the back," Big BD voice blares through the deck of men. As everyone exits their cells heading to the dayroom, I'm thinking to myself, *All this over some fucking chocolate cakes,* or should I say it's over principle—you be the judge.

"So is this everybody?" CM suggests."

"Yes, say what you gotta say."

"Okay We not even gonna open this up with a prayer or nothing. We are only here to address a greedy nigga, whoever runs the Nation Box step in the circle. This whole time I'm watching Lil Cliff's greedy-ass body posture because he knows we're here for his actions. BD, I see you got yourself down for four of the cakes. Where are they?" CM suggests.

Cliff answers, "I—I ate them, but I'ma put them back on commissary day. I also two-for-one myself."

"Where does it say that you two-for-one yourself on this paper, because I sure don't see it." Cliff stands there quiet as a church mouse, knowing it's tight on his ass.

"This is exactly what I be talking about when it's all about you, and fuck the guys." So you ain't think none of us wanted a cake, huh?"

A silence. Cliff knows he has no way out of this situation, so his lips remain sealed shut.

"Big BD, come here," CM calls, as we begin to huddle. "Tell them to beat his ass one minute, cover-up."

"Hold on, hold on," I interfere. Why he can't just do a seven-twenty full exercise instead of beating on the brothers?

"What?" CM says to me, disappointed as if he was my big brother preaching the word. "See, that's the problem. You don't get it, Lil folks. These niggas-well, *all* niggas don't understand shit until you beat it in them. You can talk all day till yo' lips fall off yo' face, and they still ain't heard shit you said. All we understand is violence, you hear me, nigga? Violence. Men were built off armies and gangs; soldiers have to be lead from the front not pushed from behind, remember that shit, and you'll be all right. If you bogus, you getting blasted. Ain't no passes for nobody; nobody's safe around this bitch, simple as that." he say, walking off.

Big BD then took the bad news back to the circle, and greedy Cliff's one-minute cover-up savage beating begin.

Damn. CM getting niggas beat the fuck up over cakes and shit already. This nigga is sick with no antidote. All he knows is gang shit; ya heard me. He something else, to say the least. The man won't even crack a smile or rarely ever joke with anyone but me and one of my New Breed partners (Big Jimmy).

Quick intel: Big Jimmy is a Field Marshall from out west, meaning he's the most powerful Black Gangster aka New Breed in the Cook County Jail currently. But you'd never know, because he's the total opposite from CM's chaotic ass. His smooth talking and long silky hair indicate that the Mac himself was somewhere in his persona, but the enormous tattoo on his right arm, of a hand throwing up "New Breed triple LLL's Treys," assures me that he's one of the soldiers, and we rocking Treys both ways for sure.

A jack-of-all-trades if you ask me, but to these cricket-ass people he's just another alleged murder suspect who's right back in jail fighting yet another murder case. Fucked up, right, but when you in the streets this the type of shit that happens, and the end result is, either you go under the earth forever, or you land yourself in these types of places; no other way out, period.

Anyway, Big Jimmy put me up on a lot of game and kept me on my toes, all while he and CM both hot as fish grease by my side daily, running shit over as they go. These two shot callers on fire, and the whole jail, possibly thousands of inmates, know where these men are or trying to find out, not to mention it's a smoked-out green light on CM and we not even knowing.

"Jimmy Sellars, you made bond," the guard yells. And just that fast, Big Jimmy is out once again, doing him. The very next day he is back at the jail, visiting me and my other Breed partner, Geno. Big Jimmy walks in looking real pimpish, with a shiny, jet-black waist-length mink. The silky fresh perm stretches his hair down his back, all while draping in diamonds and gold. I admire the look of success and the priceless shit-talking he preach to me.

I learned a lot from Jimmy, in a short time and applied it to my everyday move about in here. I stand strong through the whole jail with no spot. I'm what you call an Outstanding Member. I move only by law, even though I'm fresh to this jail shit. At this moment, me not understanding the power I inherited by just being in the presence of CM and Big Jimmy, put me at a disadvantage to niggas. I never gave a fuck about no status shit, but these two men got my face card, hot as fish and grits around this bitch, and I don't like this dangerous ass attention.

RIP Big Jimmy

V

(It Wasn't Us)

Being on point is mandatory, as well as necessary for me when en route to see the judge. Can you imagine, thousands of wild-ass niggas going to court, all piled on top of each other, in this hot-ass bullpens? At this very moment, we all feel like wild growling pit bulls crammed in a kennel, with no food. So trust and believe, niggas ready and willing to beat on a nigga head over any little thing.

"Got damn, who the fuck is that smelling like a sewer?" a loud voice blares from a tall slim guy standing a few feet away. "Hold this, hold this square," he suggests to his partner, then proceeds to direct the play with one hand, while covering his nose with the other. "Grab that nigga laying there smelling like a sewer," he calls out.

"Hell, naw, I gotta go to court too," his partner quickly responds, looking disgusted as well. They both hovered over old school, while he laid on the floor, substituting a pillow with a roll of tissue. The next thing I hear—"Wash yo' ass, wash yo' stankin' ass"—then they begin kicking and stomping old-school's ears together while he make a quick ball of himself.

You can hear the man's head crushed against the floor, as his muffled screams of help fall on deaf ears. "Enough, enough," another guy interferes, and the stomping is over in mid-kick, but old-school ain't come out that turtle shell until the coast was crystal clear.

"Personal hygiene is law," the shot caller sneers, still towering over his victim. From what I can see, this is just an indication of pain, hurt, and violence that flows through these men's veins, but don't get me wrong: it's a few cats in here happier than a sissy with a bag of dicks on Mothers day.

As the crowded bullpen simmers down, out of nowhere an aggressive voice blares, "What's up, BD?" while greeting me with the clenched fist.

Who the fuck is this fat stomach lil nigga? I'm thinking, as my antennas go up, instantly ready for whatever. "What's up?" I reply.

"I know who you are. You over there with CM, right?" he asks.

"Yeah, why? What's up?"

"Folks on some bullshit. He ain't doing BD," he says irately. "I also got a kite from Tory, but give it to whoever's in play over there, just not CM." I take the kite and cuff it, as I continue watching Lil Fatso as well as my surroundings. "You got a square?"

"I don't smoke," I answer, irritated at this point, so he backs off a little but stays posted by me until I get up outta there.

It's so weird to me because I never seen any of these niggas in my life. Plus, I have no spot. But my face ringing among killers and alleged killers in the zoo, but it is what it is. You either ride or die, and I'm riding till the tires burst and the wheels fall off this bitch with my side.

Despite all of the BS and distractions going on around me, thoughts of us going home today over-cloud my head as I enjoy the long walk to court. As soon as we make it to the courtroom bullpen, curious me bust the kite down in the bathroom. "Ain't no nigga bigger than the mob"; he a guest in my house. This my jail. "Sit him the fuck down, or everybody's head on the chopping block over there." *Damn, he talking nuts,* I chuckle while pissing on the kite and watching it flush away like a piece of shit. *Fuck all that. We got enough on our plate already, so fuck that kite* is my exact thoughts and actions.

"Dotts, Colton, attorneys," the guard yells. As I approach the bars I'm greeted by a heavily breathing, balding, badly dressed white man fumbling papers. "Hi, Mr. Dotts." "I'm public defender Robert Claxton, and I'll be looking after your case till further notice, so be patient."

"No problem" I reply.

"Okay, good, so this matter will be continued until the twenty-third of April. Do you have any questions?"

"No," but before I could say another word, our conversation is abruptly disturbed by AZ and his lawyer, having the same interaction, but heavy on the spice. ("Get me the fuck outta here." "Damn, another Buck Rogers." "Go put a motion in for dismissal or something," AZ screams loudly at his lawyer. "It ain't even Christmas yet. *Fuck*," he pouts.) I guess breaking the bad news to AZ about the continuance has scared the shit out of my attorney, sending him running, and dropping papers to the back. Strangely to some, it never bothers me that we rarely step a foot in the courtroom, but I figure I'm here now, so I'm prepared to sit for however long it takes, 'cause we still got a chance. After the smoke clears, we are later returned to our units in silence, and I just lay it down for the rest of the day.

VI

Time

Seventeen, 18, 19. —Clack-clack-clack. The loud popping of the interlock gate and screams of "On the new, on the new!" alerts me mid–push-up that yet another man has entered Cook County Hell. From afar I can see a young black, 120-pound lil nigga, give or take, walking towards me draping in a big ass 2x DOC fit. It seems to me he's been laying around on floors from the looks of his woven matted nappy hair, which I noticed before he turned into his cell. Without a minute passing by, Big-Clothes Shorty was back out the door, darting swiftly to the empty phones. *Damn, another young brother that's gonna learn a cruel reality real quick, especially fucking with them phones,* I'm knowing.

At this point, I'm kinda tired, but I make it through the rest of my sets and head to the shower. In passing, one of the guys confirms Big-Clothes Shorty BD from the hundreds. *Okay, cool,* I think as I keep it moving in pursuit of some hot water. After I hop out the shower, I can hear Big-Clothes Shorty on the phone overly aggressive to whomever he's talking to. Me thinking nothing of it, I continued rushing to lay it down, feeling relaxed and refreshed now.

After maybe an hour or so of just laying here, it never fails: a *tap tap tap* at my bars awakens me yet again. "BD, check it out."

"What's up, I say, kind of pissed these niggas wake me again.

"Come meet one of the guys from the hundreds. He on the new."

"I know, I'll be out there in a second." After I strap down and exit the room, I see one of the BDs flagging me from Big-Clothes Shorty's cell.

"Bless this house," Shorty greets and salutes me as soon as I enter. "What's up, Folks? I'm Lil Fred. Where you from?" There's confidence in his tone, although I hear different.

I'm from the Gardens," I answer while chuckling at Shorty, but return the same question back his way.

"I'm from the eight ball, 108th, down the hill," he says.

"What they grab you for?"

"They grabbed us for a bogus ass murder, that we ain't have shit to do with."

"Oh, you got a rappy, huh?"

"Yeah, but he ain't over here with me. On BD we up out this bitch though, asap." Lil Fred goes on and on about his beliefs of getting released soon, so much that I can't take another word.

"Okay, Lil Folks, I hear you," I say, chopping his sentence

in half, and exit the room, gladly regaining my hearing. "You know where I'm at. Holler at me and tell them people to come get you out that big ass DOC fit.

What Lil Fred don't know: you either bond out this bitch or park your flesh 'cause ain't nobody just getting outta here without putting in the time and going through the process.

Later that night after dinner trays rolled, and most of the guys scattered doing them. Some playing cards, some cooking, some exercising—you know, keeping themselves busy, but reader, take a wild guess where Lil Fred is? Yep, just like you thought, Gorilla-glued to that damn phone like broken wood, not to mention, he loud as hell on top of that, but who can blame him?

However, riding the phone is all good and dandy as long as nobody else wanna use the motherfucker. It's rules that need to be followed in doing so. This shit comes with the respect that your men and others will demand, so if niggas don't wanna clash like the Titans,

every mob must stand on their own people for their actions, point blank period, or your opposition will; simple as that.

"I was at home on BD, they put this shit on us," Lil Fred screams, freezing the whole dayroom mid-activities. "WTF," Big BD mumbles, hopping up and heading in Lil Fred's direction, pissed. Just as Lil Fred is positioning his bath towel back over his head for privacy, Big BD yanks it off. A startled Lil Fred looks up in shock.

"Nigga, if you can't lower yo' motherfucking voice on this phone, don't pick that bitch up no more."

"I wasn't even loud, folks," Lil Fred says, still kinda resisting Big BD's words.

"You heard what I said. I know you better not raise your voice no fucking more on this phone." Big BD tosses Lil Fred's towel back on his head, leaving him to his conversation.

Me and Lil Folks continued playing cards as a disgruntled Big BD disappeared to the back. After about an hour or so of me skunking shit on the card table, Greedy Cliff approaches and taps the table, looking disturbed. "We in the back," he says and gestures, "come on." *Here we go*, I think, rising to my feet, because I definitely know how an emotional man looks when there's a problem.

As I approach, most of the guys huddle up by my door cross-talking. "What's up?" I ask.

"Folks, I knew something was up with that lil nigga on the phone," Big BD states, pacing back and forth in my cell.

"What you talking about, that phone shit?" I ask.

"No! That nigga Lil Fred is in here for killing Lil Yummy," Greedy Cliff says while holding the bars, shaking his head in sorrow.

I damn near choked on my own words saying, "Get the fuck outta here. Who told y'all that?"

"The vent and some of the folks from upstairs said Lil Fred in here for doing that to Yummy," Cliff says, still with his head down.

"You bullshitting." I cringe, still trying to grasp what I'm hearing.

"That's why that lil nigga screaming on the phone like he crazy, 'cause he in here for that bogus-ass shit. It all makes sense now," Big BD sternly states, still pacing the floor.

CM says, "Come here," and Greedy Cliff tugs away at my shoulders. I instantly walk off with a few guys, trailing definitely, feeling different about the sprung news I just received about Lil Yummy.

Tap, tap, "Bless this house. What's up? You know Lil Folks that just got here?"

"I know, I know," as I cut CM off in midsentence, "they just told me."

"Wasn't Lil Folks ten or eleven years old?" He sounds kind of agitated by the fucked-up news he received as well.

"Yeah, he was eleven. Either way, that shit bogus. "Bogus ain't the word, but tell Lil Folks to come here when he gets off the phone. We need to see what's to this nigga story—and don't let him call back when he hangs up."

"Check it out, Lil Folks, come here," says Big BD, flagging Lil Fred down from the hall, catching him in mid-redial.

"Lil Fred hangs the phone up and begins slowly walking our way, looking nervous and feeling unsure as to why Big BD calling him to the back at this moment. "What's up, Big BD?" he says before entering the hall.

"We need to holla at you real quick," CM says. "Come here." At this moment I know Lil Fred wishes he had a magic broomstick so he can fly away, but ain't no such thing; these brooms only for going across a nigga's head in here.

The fact that Lil Fred knows his cover's blown makes him slightly pause before entering, thinking the worst. "What's up, BD?" he says as if he gathered himself not to sound or seem weak.

"So you in here for killing Lil Yummy," a towering CM says. "Folks on BD, hell no, we ain't do that shit, on my Granny we fina' be up out this bitch.

"Where yo' rappy at?" CM questioned, attempting to box this situation in.

"He in the Audy home. He only fourteen, so I don't know, but we up out this bitch, watch: they put this shit on me, on BD."

I'm just sitting here looking at the lil nigga, 'cause I know me and my rappy's in here for some shit we ain't do, so it's possible. But this one right here, I just don't know. "Okay, li'l folks," says CM, "I hear you, but we gonna play this one close." With that, he releases Lil Fred from the twenty-one questions.

At this time, I'm taking all this shit in amongst CM and Big BD. "Folks, they did that shit, you can tell," Big BD blurts out with no hesitation.

"I don't know, but the fucked-up thing about this is, I was just seeing that shit all over the news right before I got here, not to mention Lil Fred and the pussy that's testifying on my case, BDs from the same area. That's fucked up. Y'all got some shit going on out there. I told you about them BDs from the hundreds," CM giggles out. "I'm just bullshitting, but on the serious note, watch lil folks's ass until this unfolds because somebody knows something, and he better hope."

"I should beat his ass. They did that shit," Big BD suggests again while exiting the room.

As the days move along, Lil Fred can see and feel the BDs ain't fucking with him, in no shape, form, or fashion, nor is a hand being laid on him, despite the allegations against him. We definitely focusing closely through a bifocal lens on his ass. Even though all the guys wanna beat that boy to death, everyone stands down. The reason being is no one knows the truth but them. It's not that we really give a fuck about Shorty; that's just how politics goes when structure in play. Now with that being said, bogus niggas do bogus shit, habitually, so his ass better not breathe too loud if he smart, 'cause these boys just sitting back making sure he doesn't do shit wrong. Quite frankly the guys bloodthirsty and looking for any excuse to do that to Lil Fred, and age doesn't matter: you in *Cook County Jail Division 1, nigga* where Protective custody don't exist.

With every day that moves forward, Lil Fred pretty much ride the phone, eat his meals, and go back to his cell and stay there. The overly frustrating situation that he's facing is a high-profile fuckup, but nobody cares, except these white folks who trying to give him a hundred years, and the niggas who quarterbacked that bogus-ass play from the shadows.

"Strap him down, grab his legs, grab his legs, strap it!"

"Awww, let me go," I scream as officers stuff me in a freezing steel chair and wrap my legs with thick leather straps, shocking my jumping nerves to a straight line. ("Hold him, hold 'im!") "Let me gooooo! Help, Mommaaaaa!" I scream as my head gets strapped to the chair as well. "Please, noooo!"

"You've been sentenced to death by the way of—"

Clack clack clack. The loud popping of the interlock gate wakes me out of my nightmares, and just that fast Lil Fred was slipping off the deck in wee hours of the morning. He definitely escaped because it wasn't looking good for him on this deck with the allegations he was facing.

Rest in Peace: To Natasha, Lil Yummy, and Kato: Too Much for This Cold World to Take Ended Up Being Fatal.

VII

Back to Back

Knocks on my bars early morning from CM with a half head of braids. "Lil Fred walked himself or something last night, huh?"

"I don't know, but I know he got outta here wee hours," I say, giggling. "What—you getting your hair twisted for a visit?"

"Yes," he replies, happy as hell, and just that quick the thought of a visit makes me think about my family.

The only link I got to the outside world at this time is Missy for sure. I love and miss the rest of my family dearly, and vice versa, but I never see any of them. My oldest sister Tangy drives down from time to time to see me, and since she coming from another state, she's able to visit any day of the week, but as far as anybody else in the family, that's it. All three of my sisters, my mother and brother help me and my mental the best way they can, but I only see two of them.

Imagine this: one day Missy chooses to bless her little Big brother with her presence, and I'm excited to see her as well;

it's been a minute. Somehow, some way, me and CM gets called for a visit at the same time. While sitting around waiting to be called out, we see a few niggas that are housed under the five-point star sitting as well, but it's all good. Even though my mind is in another world, I notice CM keeps looking in their direction, and I can just imagine the look on this nigga face.

"Dotts," the officer yells, "booth three." I walk in and sit anxiously as Missy hit the corner, smiling from ear to ear. My heart melts with joy. She's my number one fan, and I'm hers as well. My protector, my backbone, my big sister, my everything. Pretty much all I have currently, in this cold world.

"I miss you so much," I preach as her mirrored words make me feel like a kid again in her presence. I tease her about her chubby cheeks as if she's pregnant.

As we talk and giggle away for maybe five minutes or so, "A nigga gon' die bout this BD shit," CM shouts while hopping up out his seat, pointing two niggas down that's out they seats as well.

I don't know what's going on, but I'm on my feet like everybody else—"'Ey, bitch, wad' up, nigga? Come on, wad' up?" Before a punch can get throwed, just that fast police intervene, cuffing and escorting all parties involved, shutting down visits asap. Damn, I didn't want my sister to see me like this, but she knows me, and she also know this gang shit can pop off any place, at any time and I ain't budging for shit.

That's some bitch-ass shit that could've waited, but that's the type of time CM on, 24/7, BD or nothing. It doesn't matter what it's about; you ride with yo' side and figure that shit out later. Even though the sight of Missy on the other side of that, glass getting escorted out with a look of terror on her face rubbed me the wrong way, when you are in jail, M.O.B. over everything. It's just the nature of the business, but I never imagined she would see the person I'm becoming. The fact of the matter is, she was watching her baby brother grow into a hardened man. Yes, I'm salty about what just happen, but that's like a rice grain on a mountain compared to the bullshit we face daily.

"No, no I don't, I don't wanna be here is all I know, especially for another nigga case, but I have no choice at this time cause ain't no doors magically opening around this bitch, and these people out for blood." So as the fight continues for my life, every day a shit, shower, and shave, but most importantly, mind my business and stay strapped. You must always stick to your people and never, I mean never, wear shower shoes in the dayroom; the deck can go up at any time. It's a thin line between hate and more hate in this bitch, so follow these rules, and you have a chance to make it out alive.

Clack, clack, clack, clack. The sound of loud steel doors popping at the break of dawn shakes me out of my doze. I hop up, strap down my shoes and my safety, and I'm out the door. This particular morning kites flying with the breakfast trays.

BD, check it out: one of the GD tray workers calls me to the bars."Here grab this kite." As I secure it, I noticed it's labeled to me, but once again, Im not the fucking kite man. I swiftly walk back to the table and nibble on the crap in front of me but not feeling it, so I dump it, jetting to my room immediately.

I'm itching to see what he has to say to me, so I aggressively tear the kite down and read it. "Blast CM ASAP, or all the BDs over there in violation for disobeying a direct order" from Tory. *Please, peace, be still, here we go with this bullshit again.* I exhale out my nose. Once again, CM already informed us of the incident that got him violated and banked over here in the first place. "Ain't no double bubbles"; we not touching him, so I flushed yet another kite without mentioning it. Moreover, I answered this time, writing back ("Ain't no double bubbles"). not really giving a fuck how the dude feel, since it was labeled to me, plus I don't know him anyway.

Although Tory's name carries weight in this bitch, that has nothing to do with me, if he not honoring *law*. The fucked up thing about this, is he sending me kites to carry out his orders on CM, like I'm his fucking go-to man, knowing CM could get both of us killed in this bitch if he wanted to. Despite the facts, Tory still pushing the issue about this is his fucking jail over everything, and what he says goes. Me not knowing the true facts or ins and outs about the situation, how am I supposed to act on it, other than what I'm displaying? Either way, I'm not touching nobody or getting nobody touched—period.

VIII

The Waffle House

As time waits for no man, we all pretty much feel like hostages growing older by the second in here. It's so stale that most of us find ourselves trying to sleep this time off or whatever we can do to cope, cause these County bars, biting bodies, to the gristle and most niggas cant take it, so trust and believe misery is a understatement for most as we thug our days and nights away.

Early morning, just waking up from a comatose sweaty nap, when the scream "On the new, on the new!" blares from up front. I hops up asap to check it out. I enter the dayroom to at least sixty eyeballs including mine racing to the quarter gate. *This nigga looks familiar*, my eyes told me. "CM, hold on," I suggest with squinting eyes. I zoom in on him like a hawk from up top. I know this ain't that pancake-ass nigga Zone from the hood. "He GD now, flipped from BD; he been all type of shit though," I mumble to CM.

"Yeah," he replies, with raised eyebrows and a devilish smirk on his grill. He in here for killing one of the Folks from the land, and trust me, he shysty like that. I know him personally. CM antennas instantly go up, grabbing both of my shoulders. "Come on," he says as we trail Zone from afar to his room.

CM ups his knife and yanks open the door, and we flood in like a hurricane on a bad day, catching him putting his things away. (Aww.) A startled Zone leaps on top of his bed, hands forward with a heaving chest, pleading, "Wait, wait, wait!"

"Nigga, did you kill a BD?" CM firmly suggests.

With eyes as big as golf balls he replies, "No, no, I ain't do that. No, I swear. Wait—it wasn't me," damn near crying a river. My mouth never utters a word as Zone stares me down.

"Nigga, let me find out, you killed a BD," CM says through clenched teeth, pointing his knife directly in Zone's face, before we exit the room.

Now that Zone can breathe again, I know we gotta play him close from here on out. I'm standing here just thinking about all the snake shit I know Zone has partaken in the hood. Then CM leans in with his devilish tone and whispers, "We fucking him up. It's yo' call though."

"No doubt," I reply, but I'm not even on that. I'm just merely letting him know the intel on the nigga like I'm supposed to, but once again he doing what the fuck he wants, and I'm right here with him.

A quick insight into the laws of Cook County Jail: Nothing or no situation from the streets applies in jail, with no exceptions but "status"; everything else is supposed to stay in the world, no ifs, ands, or buts about it. Do the rules get broken here and there? Yes, but law is law, and no man above that. Trust and believe though, when it does get broken, heads on the chopping block for sure.

Let's be honest. I'm knowing if I wasn't around this dude, he'd most likely be dead by now because I deflect a lot of shit off him. And the sad part about it is, he probably doing the same just for me; ain't no telling. Sad to say, as the two heads' beef festers on they both draw an invisible line in the sand and trust this shit ain't to be crossed, but when you dealing with two habitual line steppers, it's always going to be some shit at the end of the day.

IX

The Curse of Clarice, Education By Fire

Loud chatter and excitement ooze from some men and their body postures, as I peek out my bars and glance at my surroundings. Me being in my own world, not trusting nothing or no one, got me thinking. *What these niggas all giggly and happy around this bitch for?* I'm doing BD all day every day; ain't shit funny this way at all.

CM taps on bars and enters excitedly. "BD, they throwing a movie on in a second—*Silence of the Lambs*. Get ready, and grab yo own snacks, "straight up."

"Yeah," I reply, spirits feeling a lil better just that quick, 'cause I never see this nigga happy about shit, not to mention I haven't watched TV in so long. I have no idea what's going on in the world, but today is different, I see.

Yes, yes, yes, they showing a movie. This should be good, and it's coming on in a few. Oh, so this is what got everyone geeked up, huh?—rotating cell to cell preparing snacks and shit. Me and CM speedballing getting ready, because we need front-row action for this one. So we rush and end up being the first and only ones in the dayroom, sitting right under the TV relaxing like we at the Marcus Theater.

"Go put yo' shoes on." It's Billy Stone, breezing by speaking to me in a muffled voice.

"What? Man gone on," I reply, clueless to his words, as he keeps it moving to the back.

Although I don't know the meaning, it means something, I just know. But at this time I'm feeling like Kendrick Lamar— please don't kill my vibe—with my legs propped up, sitting patiently in my own world. "Gimme some chips," I ask greedily.

CM responds with his lips twisted, "Nigga, eat ya own shit." It's funny, man run them chips.

Maybe a minute or so later, out of nowhere, *bong!* A loud crushing sound echoes off the back of CM's head, sending him flying under the TV like a dud skyrocket in the dirt. My split-second reflexes let me know somebody then got up on us.

Sword already in hand, I spin around in disbelief—what the fuck? My heart beating out my chest with pure terror staring at the crowd on the attack, with murder in their eyes. Trapped in the corner under the TV, I'm swinging my knife wild and viciously while screaming, "What the fuck y'all doing? Back up!" as airborne mop ringers, chairs, and mop sticks crunched our bodies from head to toe with little resistance.

As trickled blood and sweat beads obscured my vision, with no time to wipe a drip, two aggressors lunged forward frantically screaming, but a swift swing from my choked knife bloodies one's bicep. Immediately the favor is returned, and I'm howling in pain from the hot ice pick melting in my back from his partner.

I glance down at CM lying at my blood-soaked Nikes, shaking like a crap game, as if he having seizures or some shit, out cold with a mouth and face full of blood. Painted red, and leaking, the alleged killers stand over him and slam lead repeatedly in his body. My whimpered kicks dished out to help CM do no just.

Buckled in an eight o'clock stance, I cringe from the overly shocking pain, as more steel is drilled in me as well. I'm screaming, but I know I can't go down, or it's over, so I'm crouching like a tiger, holding on to the bars the best way I can with one hand, inches away from passing out. On top of that, I got noodle legs and slipping on CM's blood. *This can't be it,* as visions of my own demise play out in real time, while I'm helplessly watching the alleged killers slit CM's throat in slow motion.

A real bloodbath. The bloody sight tattoos my brain. But on the flip side of things, everything is moving in slow motion—slow enough to notice one face I'll never forget in the midst of them killing us. Zone—yeah, GD Zone. Before brightness overcame me, I see his shysty ass throwing shit, as well as others.

This is right up his alley on the get-back side of things. *Damn, I should've listened to CM* crosses my mind for a split second as we being left for dead. Dead or alive is the question; I really don't know, because I don't see any heaven or hell, but what I do see is my whole life, flashed in clips in front of me. The good, the bad, and the ugly, all the way from childhood to current.

"Perry, Perry, get up. It's okay, son," Grandad assures me, as my battered body blankets CM, bleeding out together. "Perry, get up." Grandad speaking again, but firmly this time, as I slightly regain consciousness, getting bobbled out on a wooden stretcher, then thrown on the back of some type of motorized vehicle like a sack of potatoes being zipped away. Destination, Cook County Hospital Emergency Room.

A real "education by fire," and we definitely caught the flaming end of the stick. Thank God, they only robbed me of the new Air Ones on my feet and not my damn life, although they tried. At this time I'm still leaking, blacking in and out, but wake back up in the Emergency Room with my black wrist and ankle cuffed to the bed.

I mumble in pain, as my body goes into convulsions getting hose stuck up my nose, as well as busting through my stomach and penis. "Y'all killing me; I can't breathe!" I'm panicking, trying to scream, but too weak and sore and most of all confused to the third power.

"Shut that shit up, nigga. Yo' ass still breathing," a tall, black, bald-face guard hovers over me and says, "You made yo' bed; now lay in it. You young street punks kill me—like y'all so fucking tough. You see where tough got yo' narrow-minded ass, don't you? Bitch, you were inches from death. I wish they would've dusted your ass off, wasting my fucking time babysitting, matter of fact."

"That's enough, that's enough," the doc says, interrupting the cricket cop tirade as my body twitches with anger from his verbal judo. "Calm down, calm down. You're gonna be okay, calm down." Comforting, soothing whispered words in my ear assure me everything will be fine, but how I'm thinking to myself, *How?*

"Mr. Dotts, do you have any kids?" Doc asks.

"No," I whispered.

"And good luck with that" are his next words before exiting the room swiftly. As I lay in pain and discomfort, with tears flowing to my ears, all I can do is reflect on my grandad's teachings and pray in my head, because I know I made this bed I'm lying in.

"Why me, Lord? Why?" but at the same time, "Thank you for still allowing life in my body." The thoughts of what I can remember are on constant rotation in my head like my least favorite song. I'm trying to make sense of it all. Why would the GDs and Latin Folks try to kill us? is the question. I don't get it.

At this point, I definitely don't know what's going on with this situation or my body, but I'm in so much pain that I can barely move and sort of wheezing with every breath I take. Not to mention, this bed soaked from me sweating, and I'm freezing under this thin-ass sheet.

Damn these niggas; then put me down for real. Four stabs to my back, one in my head, and one in my rib cage, as well as a bruised, beaten, and bloody body. As Father Time ticks away, the real question is *How long have I been in here?* but I refuse to ask, 'cause honestly, I'm scared of the answer. I gotta get outta here, but I know I'm not ready because I'm fucked up, not to mention they did CM worse. So dead or alive is the question about him, and truthfully speaking I have no idea at this time.

"Mr. Dotts, how are you feeling?" Doc appears outta nowhere, shaking me of out my daze.

"I'm breathing, Doc. I can't complain."

"Well, Mr. Dotts I got good news and bad news."

Here we go. "Shoot, Doc, what you got?"

"The good news is that you're blessed to be alive after a vicious attack like that, and I'm very sorry that this has happened to you. The bad news is you'll be sent back to jail shortly." And just that fast I was on the next rocket flying back to the Cook County Jail.

X

Play Stupid Games, Win Stupid Prizes

No sooner than my feet touch the boulevard in Division 1.
"Dotts, you okay?" Officer Langley asks, wiping the sweat
beads off his perspiring big head.

"Yeah, I'm cool," I reply.

"It sure got ugly up there. Be careful, son—and oh yeah,
CM breathing," he says. "You saved his life." *Ain't that some
shit*, I'm thinking as I pimp off. *We just survived a death
violation and CM feels I saved him.* Damn, you think my face
was ringing in the zoo before. Max that out now; it's on.

"Dotts, B2," the guard says, unlocking the door.

"Y'all funny. You rotten-ass people gonna send me right
back to the same deck they just tried to kill us on."

"It's not my call," he replies with a shrug. I then begin
climbing the stairs slowly, hunched over, because my body is in
so much pain, but the fact I'm knowing I can't let these niggas
see me defeated angers my soul, and I straighten my shit up as
if I never got touched.

When I yank open the door and come through the gate, all activities pause in amazement. Niggas look puzzled like they staring at a ghost, and I stare back angrily. A few pussies got banked around, but it's still most of the niggas here that was with the hit. Im pissed off that I can't do anything physical because I'm broken up and outdone. Although I wanna body these cowards, I gotta move right. This shit is really chess and checkers, so I'll get up with them on the rebound, because I understand get-back comes with time.

All my real guys are gone, so I'm just sitting around my cell for forty minutes to an hour, not trusting shit. *Y'all gotta kill me* is the only mentality I have.

Miserable and tired of just laying around on one side of my body, I hop up and stick my head out the door, and look who I see. BPS (Billy Stone) slid past me once again, but this time with a face of sorrow and disappointment. "I tried to warn you. I told you to put your shoes on." (*Oh shit*, as I reflect!)

"You definitely did," I replied, "but me being blinded and distracted at the time, worrying about a damn movie—I knew it meant something. Damn, I fucked up, it completely went over my head. You tried to save me. I owe you one."

"No doubt. Be safe."

"You too," and then he was gone yet again.

XI

Returning a favor

"Dotts, Cermak," the officer yells from the bubble. Yes, some well-needed air for me and my bruised and battered body.

I instantly leave the deck to be greeted by CM and the lieutenant on the boulevard. "I see you alive," I poke.

"Yeah, you good," he slowly mumbles with a big white, slightly soaked gauze covering the right side of his neck, that now houses thirty-eight staples, from the bottom of his chin to the top of the collar bone. Geesh. We slightly embrace, and his next words are "Liu, get him over here with me."

"Go pack yo' shit," Liu humbly tells me. I had nothing, so I was in and out like a robbery, right back with CM (Clinched Fist).

Clack, clack and the door pops. When I enter the crowded dayroom, I'm escorted through the onlookers to the back by two BDs. While approaching, I can see almost everybody with T-shirts over their profiles with grown man hands wrapped with ace bandages. I'm knowing somebody about to get their ass kicked 'cause the sight is oh so familiar.

Despite not knowing the play, I'm not worried a bit as I enter the three-sixty, greeting and saluting the guys as they do the same. CM instantly looks at me and then aggressively says, in his newly low-pitched tone, "Tory, step in the middle." Tory does just as he is directed. "Do you know this nigga?" CM asks.

"No," I reply.

Then he shystly says, "This the nigga that's calling bogus DVs"—death violations on BDs—while staring him down. *Call GD Big Heavy,* CM implies.

I'm thinking to myself, *You mean to tell me, this the lil nigga that tried to get us killed? Do you mean to tell me, this the nigga I've I been hearing all the gossip about? You mean to tell me, he my height and weight and causing all this ruckus in this bitch? You mean to tell me this the nigga that been sending all these fucking kites like he crazy? Motherfucker, you,* I thought, and my reflexes smacked his ass into next week like a pimp does his ho.

Although that shit hurt my body, nobody moved or made a sound. You could hear a mouse piss on carpet. Despite how I'm feeling about Tory at this moment, it just goes to show that you can never judge a book by its cover.

"Thousand pardons." Big Heavy enters the circle, ready to blurt some shit out.

"Heavy, what happened? What Tory tell you?" CM asks.

Staring straight at Tory with disgust, Big Heavy stacks it on the Boss and blurts out, "You said send CM up outta there and any nigga riding with him, 'cause you run this mafucking jail. You also said that you called the DV under the One Love Concept because you knew for a fact that the BDs weren't gonna touch him."

"Okay, enough said, good-looking," CM mumbles, and Big Heavy immediately leaves the circle shouting, "Disciple crazy," feeling accomplished.

Damn, Big Heavy stamped it in blood, leaving Tory back here with all these alleged killers, waiting on the word. It's definitely tight on his ass fo' sho', and he knows it. Poor Tory's fucked up major this time from the looks of his slouched body, standing here knowing he's guilty as two left feet.

"Silly you," CM smirks while antagonizing Tory. "You never imagined this day would come, huh? You banked on me being dead. Well, shall I say, you banked on us being dead, pussy."

"No, I—"

"Shut the fuck up, nigga. Pressure is made for strong men's shoulders, not bitch niggas' hips. Now man the fuck up."

I'm standing here watching CM growing angrier and angrier with every word he says. *What on God's green earth are they about to do to this man back here?* I'm thinking. And then all in one motion CM comes from behind his back clutching two blades, one in each hand, pointing dead in Tory's face. "Bitch, you gonna take two of these in both of your arms and legs or this five-minute pumpkin head," he mumbles through gritted teeth, like a bloodthirsty, deranged killer.

A lose-lose situation if you ask me, but well deserved.

Basically, pick your poison. At this moment the term *scared shitless* is an understatement. I know Tory would rather commit seppuku than be here, right now. The double-dutching of his words falls on deaf ears, so I'm sure at any time this man fina' fall out hollering and screaming like a five-year-old getting a whooping.

Surprisingly, Tory pushes both knives away, and just that fast he's in a full nelson, and the savage beating begins.

One, two, three ... As father time ticks away, the guys take turns beating his face in. Every blow he receives makes a loud *thud* sound, as if you beating a raw steak on the kitchen counter. Two minutes haven't even passed by yet, and the guys are sweating and dead tired. Meanwhile, Tory fucked up and unconscious, as they beat away on his mug. I gotta do something, or he'll be dead in no time. Then my light switch cuts on, and my thoughts speak to me: *Why should I give a fuck? He tried to kill us.* Then my common sense kicks back in and says, *You trying to go home, ain't you? And you know if they kill this nigga, that shit ain't happening for you.*

I'm sorta having the angel on one shoulder, devil on the other effect. So with better judgment, I immediately spring into action and take over the count—fifty-five, fifty-six, fifty-seven—and speed-count the rest of his death wish. Blow after blow after blow he takes. *I know this nigga gonna die, if he ain't already dead are my exact thoughts,* as I start skipping ten or twenty numbers to hurry up and get it over with.

"Time up, Time up!" I scream. "It's over, it's over!" The

beating immediately stops as I watch the back of his bloodshot swollen head and shit-stained DOC pants get towed away, while CM stands there looking like the devil in the flesh, staring at me.

Damn, I ain't never saw no shit like this in my life. They beat the cow, pow shit outta him. He's definitely on bunk rest for sure; ain't no question 'bout that. But he doesn't need to be here, in this condition. My mind starts fucking with me, and I'm thinking to myself, *How can this be? This is the man that tried to kill me*, but I feel remorseful for what has happened to him. *What the fuck is wrong with me?* clutters my brain, before the thoughts of "no love" take over. I gather myself, shake that shit off quickly, and keep moving along with my day.

Later on that night me and GD Rien chopping it up, and he says, "I'm fina' go check on my celly."

"Hold on, I'ma go with you," I reply, just outta curiosity. When we enter the room, I can't believe my eyes. GD Rein instantly breaks down on one knee crying, and I can see why. The sight of Tory stood my hairs up and gave me chills, goose bumps, bubble guts, and I was ready to go. *I ain't never seen no shit like this in my life.* I tell y'all, the man's whole mug is bloodshot red. His head is as big as the pillow he lies on, with tennis ball eyes, overlapping and sealed shut. His lips look like two bikes tires stacked on top of each other. Even his ears are like saucers. It's terrible.

This nigga barely breathing and needs medical attention asap if he plans on seeing another day. It's sad, but just another case of *you made yo' bed nigga; now lay in it, sleep in it.*

I exit Tory's cell prematurely to locate CM, and I find him tucked off in his room alone. "Bless this house." I enter, looking directly at him. "You gotta get him outta here or it's over for him."

"Fuck him," he says nonchalantly with his face buried in his entertainment.

I damn near jump out my body. "I'm not trying to hear that shit," I reply.

He drops whatever he was laying there reading. "Fuck him, like I said," he says, jumping up in my face. "Who you talking to?" with that harsh tone.

"You," I reply even harsher. A slight staring match ensued for a quick second.

"Then walk him off the deck, wee hours," are his last words.

"Okay, cool." Now that I got the green light to get him outta here, all this man gotta do is stay breathing until later on. The rest of the night we keep the guys posted by Tory's door. It's one a.m. and I'm sleepy as hell, but I'm making sure he gets up outta here before I close my eyes.

Knock knock knock. "Come in."

"BD, I need y'all to come walk dude outta here."

"When?"

"Right now," he says.

"Yes, he gotta get outta here now," I respond, and they are up, linking with security already at Tory's door. The guys pick his limp body up, throw a bed sheet over his swollen-ass head, then proceed to carry him to the bubble.

"Guard, pop the gate, pop the gate. Come get him outta here," the guys yell, as they approach the bars.

"What the fuck y'all did, fellas?" the guard sighs, as an unfunctional Tory gets laid on the floor like a palette, by the BDs, who then disappear back where they came from. Damn, it's been a long day; now I can exhale and rest a lil.

Thank you, Father God, for not being ready for that man, because nobody seems to care or even have a crumb of concern about a jailhouse murder but me. Most niggas are not thinkers, and CM is a live wire, if nothing else, 24/7, so trust and believe, this ain't the first time I had to cut the light bulb on in his head about shit he already knows. The reality of it all is CM just doesn't care; he acts off pure impulse, so in most dilemmas, I gotta make decisions for him, or we all will be dead in this bitch; leave it to him. Although I feel his pain, I respect him as a man for being frontline in all situations and for never sending the brothers off to do things he himself wouldn't do.

I'll never know the true facts about CM and Tory's situation, but I picked a side, and I'm glued to it: "facts." The hunger and thrill of power collided these two heads, damn near to death. We all dancing with the devil, so I guess that's what gave Tory his own green light on us, huh? Either way, the failed DV attempt left him fending for himself in a den of wolves. Good try, but—I'm still breathing The moral of the story is to be aware of your actions because every action births a reaction.

XII

Check Out the Plot Twist

Now that the root of that problem dug up and out, and hopefully done, *What's next?* I'm thinking. The heat from Tory being beaten 98 percent to death flew through the jail with lightning speed. This led to niggas getting banked around from deck to deck. Thank you, Father God, again, for still allowing breath in Tory's body, even though I know damn well he's not deserving. Truth be told, I'm cool with it, 'cause ain't no telling who would've had my name in their fucking mouth, when it's all said and done.

"Dotts, pack it up."

"What you say?"

"Pack it up—you heard me," the guard yells.

Oh shit. As I spin back into my room to grab my belongings, the guys begin cluttering my door saying their farewells. "I'ma holla at y'all, Folks. Love."

"Let me holla at BD, y'all." CM clears the room.

"Ay, lil badass nigga," he says leaning on my bars, "we

have been through a lot of shit together, and I got love for you. I wouldn't say it if I ain't mean it. With all this shit going on, I never got a chance to thank you for saving my life, so thank you, first and foremost. I never had to question your loyalty or decision-making for the M.O.B. or as a man; you solid as they come. You know what's up with us.

"I'm on my way to the joint, so here go my sister's number. Call her if you need me."

"All good," I replied.

"Wherever you go through here, they know what's up, but you gotta watch the guys 'cause I been blasting they ass left and right around this bitch, for the bogus shit they been on. So watch the shenanigans; they know you my right hand,"

"Listen to me."

"I hear you, BD."

"Dotts, let's go," the guard yells again.

"Let me get up outta here, CM."

"Okay, cool. I ain't gonna hold you, but be safe and go home," he says, as we shake up and embrace for the last time.

"You be safe too," I reply, heading out once again, getting banked to who knows where.

"A4, Dotts, in there, A4."

Okay, cool, as I open the door and climb the stairs ready for whatever. "On the new, on the new!" From the moment the gate popped, I'm being stalked by the few dudes sitting around the uncrowded dayroom. Although it's a hallway full of noisy, nosy niggas, one of the guys spots me, and we greet and salute each other ("Check it out, BD," he says) as I follow them to a cell, not trusting shit.

"Bless this house." Upon my entrance, I'm thinking, *Where the fuck the bunks at; this looks different. Holy shit, this* is *different; it's like four cells in one.* "BD, you can come in here with me, and Lil Folks gonna go bunk up with his rappy or whatever; rearrange some shit for you."

"However," I reply, still tripping on how big this damn cell is. I set my lil shit up, way across the room as if the coronavirus was plaguing, and lay back for a second in my thoughts, reflecting on CM's words from the legendary Al Capone cell.

It only makes sense that the fake none-following Law guys lowkey gunning for me, and I ain't ducking no nigga, so until I pass that threshold, fuck 'em, I'ma continue to lay low and play slow, and straight manifest my thoughts of freedom from this mini-mansion. Al Capone was a motherfucker, I promise. *The original Windy City gangster lived in this very cell,* I think, laying here. But do this, make me a gangster because I'm gangbanged out and laying in the infamous Al Capone cell.

No, but you know what makes me a man before anything despite my fuckups? Number one, I believe in my higher power. Two, I love and never disrespected my mom and will always do right by her. Three, I have morals and integrity. Four, I'm loyal to those who are loyal to me. Five, I take care of my family and friends to the best of my abilities. Six, I've never done anything to a man that wasn't deserving. And seven, I don't prey on the weak or draw off numbers. Just a few reasons about what makes me a man before anything. What about you? A gangster is not about being tough. It's about being a man and doing right, while understanding your wrongs, owning them, fixing them, and moving on. Moral of the story: a real man is a true Gangster by nature.

Anyway, for what it's worth, Al Capone had his way, on and off the streets, from the looks of this shit. This big-ass room feels empty, and it needs some interior decorating because BD just living in this bitch. Reconstructing should be quite easy if I do say so myself, so I begin.

Every laundry day I drop my load on Whiteboy Jim. Now Jim is a tall version of Butthead from Beavis and Butthead. He does it all, but his specialty is reading and washing drawers and socks and shit. Jim has no one like most of us, so his survival is key and by any means. Many would think of Jim as a gay man, but no, it's just his hustle. He hand-washes all loads on the deck for three dollars; this is how most men's underclothes get washed. Our fresh sheets and towels come every Sunday morning, so I make sure I grab a stack of them both every visit.

Interior decorating is relaxing, as I keep laying towels all over the floor for the carpet. I melt toothbrushes to stick the sheets to my bars for my privacy, but never cover the catwalk bars, because that's where the guards walk around doing head counts. For finishing touches, I hang my pics, and now I can chill. It's way more comfortable in here now, but I want this bitch to feel like the Ritz Carlton.

XIII

Mirror, Mirror

"Dotts, visit," a guard yells. *Tap tap* on my bars: "BD, you got a visit."

"I know; I ain't crazy. I heard my name," but who could this be because I'm definitely not expecting anyone, especially not my representation. Curious, I hurry and get myself together and jet out. Damn, it's jam-packed in here like it's everybody's birthday, from the looks of things. Just the sight of niggas everywhere forced a slight chuckle to my face, thinking, *What if CM was in here right now?*

After ten minutes or so, "Dotts, booth four." When I enter booth four and take a seat, I'm anticipating who about to bend that corner, as everybody rises to their feet while the visitors pile in. Furthermore, the crowd is simmering as people take their seats when I notice a familiar white doctor jacket as well as a familiar face I know staring at me, looking lost and overwhelmed. "Son, is that you?" he says, really unsure as to grab the phone or not, so I do it for him. "Son, how are you?

You look so different, like a grown man now. I was informed through some of my colleagues about what has happened to you. You okay?"

"Yeah, I'm okay, but what are you doing here?"

"I never knew you were here until I was informed, and I would've been here sooner but been working a lot lately. So how's everything going with your case?"

"I won't know until it's that time, but anyway, long time no see."

"Yeah, you're right, and that's why I'm here. I wanna help you get outta this place, help you get proper representation, and I'll send you some money when I leave. Have you talked to the family, your mom or anyone?"

"Don't mention my mom."

"Aww, son, I just don't see where all those stories about me beating on your mom come from. Yeah, we argued quite a bit, but—" Blah, blah, blah is all I hear as he continues speaking his foreign language while I continue staring him down.

I can't believe Mr. Dotts sitting in my face lying as if I wasn't there throughout his rampages when we were kids. *How fucking dare you insult my intelligence?* I think, still staring at his lying face.

"Guard, I'm done. Take me back to my deck." Mr. Dotts, now standing as well, dropped his head and aborted his mission at once. Truth be told I'm happy to see him, but just can't ignore the lack of accountability he is taking right now for making his wife and kids' home life a scary place.

"Exit this way," the guard directs, and I'm back to my deck. Still feeling confused and drained, I just lay it down for the rest of the day.

XIV

Give It to Me Baby

As the days crawl along, it's yet another stressful one ahead, but celly up and out, due morning hours for court. So I'm just woke, kicked back, chilling, rereading some old letters and pics that I've accumulated over some time. Which leads me to blow the dust off my *Black Tails* magazine and start lusting over these fine-ass women. I haven't thought about sex in so long that I forgot if this motherfucker gets hard or not. *Oh shit, let me put this book away and get back to sleep,* my mind tells me, and in no time I doze back off.

"Aww, yes, baby," she moans. "Yes, fuck me, Daddy—don't stop" before I am abruptly awakened by some fat nigga snoring loud as hell. Still and all, I can feel my penis hard as a steel pipe, throbbing with a heartbeat in him when I grabbed the head. It's up there, and it's stuck there, so I just continued where I left off. *Smack, smack, smack.* I slowly stroke this swollen black pole up and down firmly, scaling the whole thing while staring at the infamous Lil Kim squatting poster of that fat-ass pussy she beholds between them thick ass thighs of hers.

Stroke after stroke after stroke, I can feel my muscles begin locking as my eyes close in pleasure while growling quietly. More muffled manly moans make her go faster and faster, splashing juices all over me. I can feel it rising from my soul at once, "plus Momma told me never stop until I bust a nut." I'm about to cum as my body and toes lock, while bolts of joyous squirts send me into convulsions, crippling my face like a Leprechaun as I jerk it all out on the floor and just lay there, thanking Biggie Smalls for putting her on, and in no time I am back to sleep, snoring like a baby.

XV

Man or Mouse

Lord, will these days ever change? I'm asking, because they're all the same, miserable and sketchy, not to mention could be my last. Lately, I've been staying in my cell a lot more than usual. Truth be told, I'm really just tired of everything. Although the GDs bogusly fighting each other like they on the streets, it's not my business or BD business. Amongst the brotherly brawls, my childhood homey Fool is in the mix of that madness. Me and Fool grew up in the same hood, and yes, he's another alleged murder suspect, caught up in hood politics, which landed him here as well. From the streets to the jail he gives no fucks.

Peep this. One morning I'm on my way to the shower and can hear a nigga pretty much screaming while loud punches connect his flesh and bones. In passing, I happen to peek in and can see it's Fool getting busy on somebody. I instantly step into the room. "Fool, Fool!" I scream. My voice stops his punches in mid-stride. "Fool, you already beat the man down G; let him go."

"I ain't playing with no nigga (G)," he says while gasping for air, still standing over a balled-up bloody man.

"Gone and walk that shit off, and I'ma holla at you later," I say and exit the room while Fool follows. To be point blank frankly, if the word gets off the deck they fighting amongst each other, all they ass gonna get blasted. With that being said, I told y'all, I've been laying low playing slow.

Thirty-nine, forty, forty-one, exhale. "On the new, on the new," interrupts my daily pushups while alerting a deck full of alleged killers that someone new is entering hell yet again. *Who the fuck is this?* I think as niggas sprint to the dayroom, with me following at my own pace.

"That's him, that's him," one of the Folks screams as the newbie enters the deck looking terrified.

"Bitch, you raped my Lil sister," one of the Gd's yells.

"No, it's not me, no, I'm in here for false information."

"Nigga, it is you. You got a tattoo of a red dragon on one of your ass cheeks; she told me. Fuck this, grab that nigga."

"No, no," the newbie whimpers, double-dutching his words.

"Pull down yo' pants, nigga, and let me see yo' ass, and you better pray it ain't shit on it." Scared shitless, the newbie yanks his pants to his ankles, tooting his bare ass in the air. The sight causes a sudden roar from the crowded dayroom as if it was going up with violence. I promise you'd think we were watching Martin mixed with Def Comedy Jam or something. I mean dudes falling out on the floor laughing, some running back to their cells.

It's unbelievable the things we do in here for laughter at any weak man's expense. It's all a big hoax to test a man's integrity and manhood, as well as make a mockery of him if he lets you. They definitely just did all three of them, and he can never be respected or taken seriously in here, ever. *It couldn't be me*, I think. Despite the entertaining moment, I gotta stay clear of the bullshit, let's not forget, because trouble sure loves to follow me, it seems, or is it just me?

XVI

Taxation

By this time my rappy's hearing all types of shit, and they sending kites crazy my way. They know these alleged killers wanna murder me for whatever reason; that doesn't matter. Moreover, Big C got some shit going on, still in pursuit of his *own* freedom. He pulled a power play somehow and start getting dope and weed in through the guards. I received a kite asking for my aid and assistance. Me being me, I want him out as well, to take care the business. Find Jarvus and make sure he doesn't show or tell the truth if he does show, and we got a chance in the courtroom.

The kits of dope started flowing, and we did our one-two thing through MoneyGram. Now the plot is this, whoever wanted dope had to send the money in a certain name of our choice. When the bread was received and confirmed on our end, and not a second sooner, they could get whatever they paid for. Taxation without representation is what it's called, and you know me, I'm standing on it. Although that shit expensive for a lil bit of nothing, anything that comes through these doors is a nuke to these niggas.

My motto is just gimme the money, and I'ma keep you high as giraffe pussy, no doubt. I come from this world, so I can spot a D-head from a mile away with my head down, and back turned. I hit a few who came in crying, shaking, and throwing up all night just to knock some shakes off their ass. Trust and believe, it's all type of niggas in here tooting this shit, from young to old, but seeing young dudes my age high off that shit kinda fucking my head up 'cause I'm from out south where young niggas smoke weed, not toot dope, but to each his own (*How much you got?*).

This shit pumping, so I been riding the phones lately. I'm wondering if they on to me or someone low-key snitching 'cause outta nowhere they starting to shake us down a lot, forcing me to keep the dope in my mouth when they come through. So it is what it is: niggas getting slightly wet dope, and you better believe it's still selling with no problem. I never want or receive a penny for my services; I understand the bigger picture. So finally, after the money was up, Big C was gone, bonded out after eighteen months.

As time goes on, I'm hearing Big C and Jarvus back hanging drinking Hennessy and shit, out there in the free world. I hope he on business though and not bullshitting, because we can't take any chances with Jarvus coming to court against us and simply not telling the truth. Throughout my stay here, I've had several phone calls with my real guys from other mobs and trust they wanna do him bad. But despite me feeling worse than them, I've always stressed, "Don't touch a hair on his chinny-chin-chin." Nothing can happen to him on my watch, plus I'll never talk on these county-recorded phones. So with that being said, everything's by kites and word of mouth around here, so you must stay in tune to be a step ahead if you wanna survive.

XVII

Spinach

Shit stay lit around this bitch, and I must know what's going on around me, so I sign up for Muslim service to get off the deck and check temperatures. Several hours later the guard yells Muslim service and we out the door, some of us with Qurans in hand and others with hidden kites ready to let them fly. For most of us, Muslim service is just a meeting spot for all mobs to politic, pass contraband, and call out hits, amongst other things. For others, it's a sacred place that need not to be disrespected as such, and I truly apologize for my actions, but the reality is this is just what's going on, and it's been going on well before I was thought of.

When I make it to the services, I greet and salute the guys and a few GDs. It's all kinda different mobs in here from all over Division 1, huddled on bullshit. "BD, what deck you on?" one of the GDs asks.

"I'm on D4," I reply. "What's up?" "Is the Folks up there fighting each other?" are his next words.

"I don't know. I mind BD business," I reply. He then looks away as if he don't believe me, but who gives a fuck. These guys still trying to push the One Love narrative on everybody, but not everybody on board, especially me. Although we did have the discussion with the GDs on somebody taking their Nation business off the deck. Whoever it is ain't come to the light yet, but it's pretty much out there now, and mafuckas' heads on the chopping block, so it's just a matter of time.

What the fuck going on in this place? It's a deck full of GDs and Latin Folks and Bros. Notice how I didn't mention the pussy Zone, amongst them once again. When we see each other in passing, I still never utter a word to him, but always knowing to myself a back door definitely in the making, I just gotta move my pieces on the board right.

I'm guessing he ain't for sure if I saw him in the midst of the DV, and even if I didn't see him, I know he was there. This nigga watching the shit outta me, because he knows, one slip-up and I'm on his ass, like flies on shit. Due to my trust issues, I'm extra on point as well and, side-eyeing everything moving per usual. Despite my snoozing, I'm a thinker at heart, so I'm still moving as such, so trust me when I tell you, every nigga gets caught slipping at some point or another. It's all about if the opposer capitalizes when they catch you, or you catch them.

Early morning loud rumbles after breakfast, startle and awaken me. I exit my door, to check on the guys and notice the GDs on security, at one of they own people cells. I think about Fool while all this going on but am too tired to investigate, so

I go and lay my ass back down. Later that day I learn Bluto putting hands on one of his guys. Big Bluto again, huh? He's acting exactly how his name sound. I don't know where he's from or what he in for, but he ain't bullshitting, exposing the weak.

Day after day he storms the deck bullying shit like United states of America. He allegedly already whooped two of them before I got on this deck. Big Bluto is pretty much on whatever with the oppositions as well. Stunt after stunt, time after time, I've watched him pull one with my own eyes. I mean turning the TV in the middle of programs, disrespecting people, as well as riding the phone all day and night. He on straight dummy at all times on the GD's expense, and they can't do shit about it. Well, I'ma say ain't doing shit about it. I never cared much for him personally, but that's just me. Who knows if he even like that for real, or if he bullying because he is big as Bluto, and the Folks got the Bros outnumbered. I mean this nigga standing on all the GDs necks with an iron boot though, excluding my nigga Fool. He knows Fool ah kill him or die trying with no hesitation.

Boom boom boom. "D4, D4, yo, send Bluto to the vent!" Manky G screams.

"Hold on, let me find him," one of the GDs responds.

Soon Bluto on the vent. "Ok. This Bluto, what's up, who this?"

"It's Manky G, Folks. I hear you up there putting yo hands on the Folks."

"Naw, G, who said something like that? These niggas just scary; I ain't on that, Folks, but I will beat snot outta one of they ass if they break law or get outta pocket."

"As long as you take proper protocol, Big Bluto G, you know how this goes."

"No doubt, Manky, but where these bogus accusations coming from? I need to know," he asked.

"The guys saw Zone at court, and he reported it."

"What? Zone, up here with me?" Bluto asks.

"Yeah, that's him."

"Say no more." Bluto storms off from the vent huffing and puffing, growing bigger and bigger by the second. He immediately calls the back, under the One Love concept. It's always something I'm thinking, but let me see what they got going on, as everyone else exits their room heading for the dayroom.

"We the members, under the One Love concept, bring Zone up on charges for taking in-house Nation business off the deck." *You can't be serious*, I'm thinking.

"Zone, speak your peace," Bluto states.

"I just saw a few of the Folks at court and was asked if the guys was on the deck bumping with each other, and I said yeah, 'cause I ain't wanna lie."

"First of all, Miss runny lips you been lying your whole motherfucking life." I hate Girly mouth, niggas like you. Pussy you know where you at. "Besides that, you know your bogus for taking nation business off the deck. So with that being said,

I won't *lie* to you about the consequences and repercussions for your actions."

Zone just standing here juggling his words to himself 'cause ain't nobody hearing him. A sad puppy dog–looking motherfucker he is at this moment, knowing he about to get grown man paws put on his ass. Zone, with a racing mind knowing this shit is really about to happen, takes a quick glance at me, and I make sure I have my Joker smile on for this glorious occasion.

"BD, we vote blast 'em. What y'all vote?" Bluto asked.

With a straight face, I turn and mumble, "Blast him," to the guys. I spin back around now looking dead at Zone with devilish vibes in my bloodstream. He knows off the rip that I am *returning a favor. "Blast him."*

Blast him, blast him, blast him—those words repeat in my brain. And just that fast, blows start raining from the top of his cranium to the bottom of his metatarsals. I told y'all, I'm merely just *returning a favor* as I watch them beat Zone unconscious. Then I exit the three-sixty grinning. *What a gorgeous back door*, I'm thinking to myself.

Sometimes you don't have to lay a finger on a snake, because karma ain't a bitch it's a mirror. However, he brought this on himself, so this doesn't count towards the role he played in CM's and my death violation, so if you still breathing after this bitch, nigga, I still owe you one. But this lil touchup good for you right now. This is the law of the land, and it requires this: pay attention when chess and checkers is being played. What the fuck was he thinking?

After the savage beating, they put bath towels over his head and carry him to the bars bloody. "What the fuck, man?" the guard yells and instantly pops the gate and Zone gets laid in the interlock like some carpet.

You'd think Zone getting beat the fuck up would be enough to stop or even slow down Bluto's continuous rampage, out loud, but nooo; he back to his usual tactics, forcing niggas to play cards while cheating them out loud for money. Besides his own GDs despising him, there are plenty more men that feel the sameway or worse about him.

Today is one of those days I can see, 'cause the Bros looking and moving like they woke up on the wrong side of the bed. You mean to tell me, every last one of them in the dayroom lurking around, doing shit they never do, and ain't nobody peeped shit but me, and from the looks of things, they about to kick it off.

However, Bluto and the GDs act as if they don't have a care in the world, to even notice all the Bros in the dayroom at the same time. Clueless to his surroundings, Big Bluto too busy bullying the card game as usual while the Bros take position before anybody else catch wind of what's going on.

Crack. Bluto is already smacked in the head with a mop wringer. *"It's up!"* All the GDs and Latin Folks and even a few BDs are startled by the bold and brassy move that the outnumbered Bros have pulled off. In doing so, all the Folks are forced back to the bars in retreat mode, basically piled on top of each other as the Bros attack. Anything that's not nailed down is flying in the air toward us. My candybar, aka knife, out while trying to dodge shit they throwing at the crowd. As I look around, I can see men down from both sides just that quick.

Suddenly we begin to spread our wings, forcing me to yank up a nigga by his collar who got a lil too close. I begin dragging his 110-pound ass to the shower area, while he squirms like a fish outta water trying to get away. I definitely don't wanna stab him, so I just punch and kick on him a little bit. Upon me working my hands and feet, I noticed my ghetto cousin Bub and two guys piled in the shower looking puzzled at me, like what the fuck just happened, so I release him, and he takes off running.

As the melee continues, I'm noticing the Folks starting to get too wild for the Bros, forcing them to scramble like eggs getting out of the dayroom as well. Some of them locking up three or four in a two man cell, just to get away.

Through the midst of the ruckus in my peripheral, I can see a wheel off a mop bucket just laying there. I grab that bitch and fastball it down the hall like Leroy Robert "Satchel" Paige or some shit ("He's out!") as the fastball connects to his face while he's attempting to steal home. As the chase brews on, we raid their empty rooms like the law, snatching all the bags of commissary down from their bars as well as taking everything that isn't nailed down.

"Here they come, here they come, on the inside!" voices

yell. The sound of those words sends us all into a frenzy to lock up. Them people are on the inside armed with Louisville sluggers, and they definitely going across the top of your shit if you get caught out there. After we lock ourselves down, they start snatching us out two cells at a time, as we all scream from room to room, checking on our people.

Through the scattered voices floating the airwaves, one particular voice screaming out behind my actions. "That's fucked up, Bro. One of them pussy-ass niggas threw a wheel or some shit and bust Snake's eye out his head. They came and got him outta here asap."

The news makes me hop dead up and just sit on my bunk. Damn, that's fucked up, because I know I threw that strike. That nigga Snake was cool, but war is war, and at the end of the day, I'm at anybody right now. Y'all know how this shit go: I gotta make it back to my family, just like y'all trying to, but once again I'm being banked all around this bitch.

So with violence being just about all I know at this point in time, I kid you not, my family and this fucked-up case only hit my mind in brief moments. Survival is key.

XVIII

The Biggest Picture

Thank you, Lord, for covering me as well as protecting me in this Cook County nuthouse. Despite all the bullshit I'm going through personally, we still got a chance at life, and I plan on going home from here, not the penitentiary. I never keep up with court dates, because they always jump four to five months apart, and keep in mind I got a Public Pretender, so who the fuck trying to rush into a courtroom? Definitely not me.

Me, AZ, and Big C all face the judge together every court date with hopes of going home each time. I was always told by the older cats to show the judge some respect with my appearance. So every night before court I make sure I wash my long hair, so it can draw up enough to pat-shape me a little afro outta respect for the judge, just as I was schooled.

Face to face with my head held high, I pray he can see through this shit. Both of my rappy's got paid, Black attorneys, but that doesn't matter. I guess the slow motion of the case is overly frustrating for AZ. The angered thoughts of *We ain't do shit, but still in jail* sometimes spill outta AZ onto his lawyer, whenever we go to court, and those behaviors lead them to full-fledged hollering matches damn near every time. Sad to say, but I'm a thousand percent sure that if these bars didn't part their bodies, they'd be wringing each other's necks.

Throughout AZ and his attorney handling their business, I always mind mine, while praying to the number one man, asking for the strength to face the number two man, which is Judge Greg T. Zuria. This is the man that's watching us grow into men, and possesses our get-outta-jail-free card, so the respect is definitely there.

Over time, as court dates switch up, so does my representation, but for now, an old white lady pops up every couple of months, promoting that cop-out shit, pissing me the fuck off. It ain't funny, because I can remember our very first visit. I was greeted with grinding teeth noises and the loud smacking of a phone book full of papers on the table in front of me. "Hey, Mr. Dotts," she implied, looking from under her slouched glasses.

"Yes."

"Mr. Dotts, I'm Karen Jiles with the public defender's office. I've studied your case file for some time now, and as your attorney, I'm here to inform you that I can push for twenty years with your cooperation against your codefendants. I'm sure it's in your best interest to take a deal, so I can get you back home to your family as soon as possible."

This woman is dumb as fuck, I see, as I shake my head in

sorrow. If I wanted to tell on something, I wouldn't be in jail. *"We ain't do shit,"* I answered harshly.

"Well, you need to start doing something and consider the life ahead of you, because it's not looking good for you guys." *Cop out, cop out, cop out* is all she knows; these were the only words that exited her mouth while sitting across from me, looking and sounding like a somewhat educated meth head.

"You tried," I told her, "but I ain't copping out or testifying against nobody."

She then begin piling all that junk back into her raggedy-ass folder and aborted her mission just as quickly as she came. "I ain't in no rush to go to the penitentiary fucking with you, lady. I'll see you in another six months," I blurted on her way to the exit. She thinking *jail time*, I'm thinking *home time*; we are not the same.

Fighting and beating my case is never a thought for these people, so the actual case is never discussed on any visit. We all looking for a *not guilty* verdict no matter who the representation is. It's already written, so I pretty much just let go and trust He keeps providing me with the knowledge to make the right decisions for my life. He shall deliver me from the presence of my enemy. I know nothing can be done without Him, including making it through this rough patch, so I try to stay prayed up for the sins I've committed and the ones ahead of me living in this hell.

XIX

The Diary

This Be The Realest Shit I Ever Wrote

"Wake up, wake up," my Breed homey Geno says, shaking me by my shoulders. "You good?" he asks while looking in the mirror, brushing his deep waves with two melted-together toothbrushes.

"Yeah, I'm good, bro, just having bad nightmares and this case starting to fuck with me." We on our way to trial shortly, and my mental stability is not so good, but I'm holding on the best way I can without jagging my bid off. I'm very content with sitting. I'll rot in this bitch before I cop out for some shit we ain't do.

Needless to say, the world moving on without me, and I can feel it, especially when certain holidays come floating around. These are the days when you can see a change in a man's behavior. "Mail run," the inmates yell, as the guard walks the catwalk throwing mail through the bars.

"Jones, Smith," the guard yells, as he goes cell to cell

distributing. I'm just knowing in my heart that I got some mail. I just need something, anything from anybody, but he always keeps walking past my cell while I sit in silence, feeling lonely and left for dead, but most of all, crushed to the core.

Nobody cares. Out of sight, out of mind is a true statement that history has proven. The family and friends you still have available in times like this, you must cherish them the best way you can. I rarely stay in contact with the family much, but may catch lil bro Ray from time to time playing some strong, compelling black powerful music. The smooth melodies and rugged baselines soothe my soul, every time I listen. Sometimes I even close my eyes, in spurts, to really feel every phrase quoted.

Tupac Shakur, the front-runner, led the evolution for our race of people through music. His real-life storytelling of our real-life events should let you know he is on the same time as us. Being born Black in a white man's world is the most realist shit he ever wrote. Institutionalized by our oppressor is just another form of modern-day slavery minus the whips on our strong Black backs. As a people, it's very scary to live Black, so you gotta be able to adapt to your surroundings in a proper manner, no matter where you are or what you're into. Unfortunately, I'm saddened to say at this time, I'm into the wrong shit and really don't know if my black ass gonna make it out of here alive.

Eye for an Eye

Many, many moons have passed us by but this particular one is full yes indeed. Me and celly up late in the dayroom playing casino by our lonely, per usual, when outta nowhere the sounds of loud screams and rumbling put our game on immediate pause. "BD, look, look it's going up over there," he says, pointing across the hall, with real conviction in his voice and face as well. Without a blink near, my pupils dialed in with precision, and in no time, we are out of our seats at the bubble being nosy—well, *cautious* I'd say, considering where we at.

Damn Folks, they dragging a nigga, fucking somebody up, and it looks like they stabbing him. What the fuck, the up-and-down motion of steel combined with the dull light from the alleged killer's knives boomerang flashes of light as if they taking old polaroid pictures. After thirty seconds or so of the savage beating, the guards close the door off, so we return to our card game, me thinking nothing of it.

For the next twenty minutes or so, all types of suited white men start to appear across the hall periodically. "On Breed, ah mafucker dead, BD," Geno blurts out, but I'm still ignoring his assumptions.

"Shit happens all the time," I reply nonchalantly.

"Yeah, it do, but a nigga dead over there," he answers with a concerned look on his face all of a sudden. "Why you looking like that Breed?" I questioned.

"'Cause, BD, either way it's gonna be some bullshit, no matter if he's ours or theirs."

"I feel you, but I got six. That's game," and I slam the cards on the table.

"I quit too," he says, still tweaking about what we just witnessed. "I'm fina' lay it down. BD, I'm telling you, they about to have that boy on a shirt in the morning," Geno states, tugging away at his own collar.

"You're probably right, but lower your voice, Breed, damn." My eyes getting heavier and heavier by the second, and this nigga still talking. "Celly on that noise a little," I repeat, "it's over."

"I got you, but let me hear this news right quick, Mr. Sleepy Man," he giggled.

"588-2300, Empire, call us today.

"In other news, a twenty-two-year-old west Cicero man, identified as Malik Strohger, was murdered last night in the Cook County Jail max Division 1, booked on simple marijuana charges. In sports, the Chicago Bears with the win over the Green Bay Packers."

Back on his feet towering over me with bulging eyes pounding his fist in his hand, "I told you. I told yo' ass," he repeated, "that's him. Damn, that gotta be him."

"You probably right," I say, undoubtedly knowing. "This cricket-ass system, damn, why they send him to Division 1 with simple weed charges?"

"Why do you think? They don't give a fuck. Now help me tie these magazines down, because ain't no telling with these niggas," Geno replies. After we locked and loaded up, my brain and body do the same, and shortly after I'm face-timing my pillow.

Clack, clack. Early dew hours, the sound of popping doors and moving bodies interrupts my nightmares, alerting me that niggas poppin' out for breakfast. So we hop up and strap down like the Navy Seals before exiting because we ain't missing a beat. As we enter the dayroom, I can just see the devilish dark cloud hovering over us as I radar the whole area with one glance, noticing the Bros from every MOB under the five posted up, walking back and forth with coats on.

We all know the business, and at this moment the tension can't be hidden. "Gimme an extra tray!" I shout to one of the Breeds.

"Ain't no extras," he responds with his hand to his mouth. "You know, a Mafia Insane got killed across the hall last night," he whispers. Damn, Geno was right. It's confirmed: the same man we saw getting murdered from afar is also the same man we heard the radio speak about up close.

I'm knowing it's on now, so I'm straight back to our table with the news. "Yo. Y'all hurry up and eat so we can get the fuck up outta this dayroom."

In the midst of the plotting, I see one of my lil neutron partners from my hood lost in the sauce. "Check it out, Parnell,"

"What's up?" he responds, with a scared, confused look on his face.

"Straighten yo' mug up, nigga. You in jail," I chastise him. "Go take the batteries out your door, and lock up now."

"Okay, okay." Without any rebuttal he was gone.

We all received the confirmed news that in fact the GDs murdered a Mafia Insane across the hall a few hours ago. Ain't no denying the Bros on bullshit, but we breezed right past them, exiting the dayroom, and kind of lurked in the hallway for a few minutes checking shit out before we locked back up. Still a lil restless, but on point, we just laid back with blades out, anticipating the bullshit.

Tap, tap. tap on my bars outta nowhere. "What's up?" me and Geno both answer, hopping up, ready.

"Y'all with that shit, BD?" Moe man speaks while huddled at my door with a few of his Bros.

"Don't fuck with ours; we ain't got shit to do with that," I respond through the bars.

"Enough said," darts out his mouth, and they pimp off down the hall. We then step back in the hallway to make sure our people posted and straight. In doing so, we see the GDs and Latin Folks in the dayroom like shit sweet, one in particular named 7.4. Back and forth, back and forth he walks in and out the dayroom provoking and wolfing indirect shit in the air towards the Bros that's already on ten.

Not to mention he breaking the number one rule: No shower shoes in the dayroom. Why the fuck do you think they call them shower shoes? because they are made to wear in the shower.

Anyway, all the above is taking place, and he knows his actions are a definite no-no, but he continues. Meanwhile, the Bros still posted and mean business, just waiting on the moment. One of they brothers just got killed across the hall last night, and they want they lick back, rightfully so.

I guess 7.4 thinks this is a game or he can't die, one or the other. Either way, he is out of his mind. No security, no shoes, no shirt, no sense if you ask me, but he is a grown man and accountable for his own actions. He knows good and well the Bros are ready to strike back with vengeance, and it's important for them to score at all cost.

As soon as 7.4 rewinds his footsteps entering the dayroom once again, the Bros pop out like Katie from around the corner, shoving a knife in his neck and shoulder, paralyzing his body instantaneously. The neck shot stretched him like a blanket, leaving him lying on his back pockets panting for dear life, like a fish outta water. With every exhale, blood darts from his neck to the ceiling, leaving red scattered freckles.

The gruesome act sends everyone into a frenzy, hollering and screaming, trying to get out the dayroom. It also forces me and my celly to duck back into our room. Lifeless, leaking, and lying there, 7.4's demise brings me flashbacks and makes me understand: it's clear that I'm here for a fucking reason, 'cause he got hit like I got hit, but he ain't fucking breathing. (Many men.)

As the murderous melee continues, the Bros all act as if they YNW Melly with murder on their minds, screaming Finball rolling. These blood-craved alleged killers aren't done at all, as they stomp like a down-south marching band to my li'l homey Parnell's cell. "Help, please, help!" Petrified screams from high-pitched vocals serenade a deck of men for this devilish occasion. With Brookfield Zoo mentality, the Bros begin climbing and aggressively yanking on the bars like real monkeys trying to get in. Parnell's celly a GD, and his head on the chopping block, leaving Parnell himself in the crossfire of death merely for just being his roommate . The two men shitting bricks, as their screams of terror only motivate the alleged killers even more. With a man down, still lying in the dayroom, begs and pleas from the balled-up men consume our ears as the seasoned killers begin throwing flaming rolls of toilet paper through the bars attempting to burn and smoke Parnell and his celly out. They want them boys dead, and I pray they can survive through this one.

Unfortunately, me and my people gotta stand down on this one: M.O.B. politics. I know the right decision was made, but damn, damn, damn; it's really a bad situation for them boys trapped in that cell. Imagine this, reader: on one hand, your room is on fire and you want out, but on the other hand, them killers on the other side of them bars and want in. Pick your poison.

Lose, lose if you ask me but after a short time, all I can hear is barking dogs,walkie talkies and chaotic screams. "On the inside, On the inside": here they come. The sounds of the crooked police and baseball bats overshadow their screams and make everyone scatter from Parnell's door and lock up. As fire extinguishers explode through the bars, we all pretty much need air from this smoky situation. Parnell and his celly are immediately yanked out of the room and rushed off the deck to safety.

A confirmed homicide, 7.4 is tagged and bagged and carried off the deck. As the bad vibes and smoke still floats from room to room in this hell, they start popping doors getting us up outta there as well. *Here we go*, I think because they at my door with them baseball bats. "Step out with your hands on your head," the officer directs. We oblige as they roughly search us down for weapons that we've already disarmed ourselves of.

As cries and laughter blend the airwaves while being escorted off the deck, it is a sad sight in passing. I never understood why, I could never see a man cry til I seen a man die. The red-soaked concrete where he laid doesn't show flowers and candles, only a yellow "slippery when wet" sign that towered over his thick, dark burgundy blood. It's a crying shame these people don't give a fuck about shit, they ain't even attempt to clean the murder scene up.

News like this shoots like wildfire through the jail and gets all the heads on the edge quarterbacking plays, so decks going up all through this bitch. It's crazy when I think about it because from afar, I saw the commotion of both men being murdered, just hours apart. "Single-file line!" an officer yells, as we're directed to move forward on the boulevard to an unknown room tucked off somewhere.

In passing you'd think we were in the Decathlon jail Olympics, because of all types of events going on, these niggas clowning, throwing up gang signs, yanking and climbing bars, as well as slinging piss and shit from bullpens, etc. Chain reactions thrive in this hellhole without a care or conscience in the world. Damn near the whole division going up in flames from what we can hear on the guards' radios, pure evil and chaotic behavior.

When we finally reach our destination, it's just an empty room with a big dark-tinted mirror on the wall. "Line up and face the glass, one cell at a time," the officer firmly states to all the inmates. My mind is everywhere at this point thinking, *Who is behind that glass?* because I know this is a lineup. *Somebody back there tricking their ass off, or we wouldn't be here,* I'm knowing. Everyone obliges with the lineup, and things run smoothly.

In and out like a robbery, but on the way to the exit, I notice something. Somebody behind that tint opened a door, and the light exposed everyone back there. Ain't that a bitch? It's like three of the Latin Folks back there pointing people out. I know they think nobody sees them, but that's their business. Later on that night, they charge Parnell and the Bros with the same jailhouse murder. Yeah, my lil homey Parnell; what a fucking shame. Parnell is an innocent man that the guards rescued from a burning room, then doubled back and charged him right alongside 7.4's killers.

This system's a joke, I mean its whole existence. How can something like this happen? It's clearly past making a mistake. A man is dead, and the newspapers clearly got Parnell's name from somewhere. I read every line they wrote in disbelief. A lot of people were hurt or died behind this melee that ripped through Division 1 this time, and for those who weren't, stay dangerous.

As time moves along, things somewhat dying down, but nothing you do in here is unnoticed, per usual. You hurt mine, I hurt yours; you kill mine, we kill yours. It's universal law, just the nature of the business for gangs; nothing personal. Everything's Laws, Policies, and Principles but, most important Power as we all know, but keep in mind every action births a reaction.

"On the inside, on the inside!" The loud sound of barking dogs from behind me, blended with screams from up the catwalk ("Shakedown, shakedown!"), alerts everyone and makes me put some pep in my step. Niggas scrambling to get rid of shit 'cause them people coming. *Ping, ping, ping.* Me and celly's arms hanging out the bars, slinging shit up the catwalk like everybody else.

All you hear is steel hitting concrete all over the place. The good thing is we run the jail, and 98 percent of the officers are here for a check. They ain't trying to catch nobody with shit, or doing nothing they don't care. Trust and believe, most only do what they gotta do to keep a job, definitely under the bare minimum at best. "Shakedown, shakedown! Please exit the cell." We exit our room while they tearing our shit up, looking for weapons and contraband, so they say. After the pat search, me and a few other guys are directed to the boulevard, but I never return.

"Dotts, they just opened Division 11. You wanna go?" lieutenant asks.

"No, no, no. The same door I walked in, I wanna walk out," I humbly reply, thanks but no thanks.

"Understood," he says, leaving me at once.

Upon standing there waiting for them to send us where we going, I notice two of the guys walking in my direction; "Treys". I greet the guys and receive silence. Okay, I think, but why are these niggas looking at me like that? I stare them both down as they keep it moving. This doesn't feel right at all. Matter of fact I know this ain't right. I'm not illiterate nigga, I can read between the lines. Just as CM warned me, I guess it's unfolding, so fuck them and feed 'em beans, like my mother would say.

"Dotts, G2," the officer directs.

"Okay, cool," I reply.

As soon as I open the door to the deck, one of the guys who took care of business on Tory approaches the bars and says, "BD, it's kites all through Division 1, to blast you on sight, move around Folks."

"Oh, the guys on bullshit, huh?" I reply. "What's they angle?"

"They say you gave the Bros a rope to tie the quarter gate down, so the GDs couldn't get out the dayroom when the deck went up."

Damn, they reaching. These niggas don't want me to be great. Tired, frustrated, and frantic, I say, "That's straight bullshit.

These pussy's trying anything to get at me, scandalizing my character. Say no more," folks, "'cause ain't no nigga touching me. Guard, get me outta here." I end up walking myself. Now I know, it's officially stamped in blood, the so-called guys on me, but I won't compromise my character for anyone.

After the shuffle of the deck—"Dotts, C4," the officer yells—when I enter this new deck, I see a couple of old heads moving about. It seems kind of laid back from the look of things. I'm greeted by a few of the guys or so-called guys, and it seems like it's love, but I ain't trusting shit with a pulse. I check they temperatures for a few, and no one mentions anything about getting me hit, and I don't either. We on our way to trial, and I need no extra shit on my plate, I promise. So I end up bunking with one of the New Breeds from out west name Yodi.

Yodi is also in for an alleged murder as well. Yodi's case is something I couldn't imagine on my worst day. Allegedly he was in some type of love quarrel. One sunny day he was visiting the woman he was dating, when shit went all bad as a tussle ensued, with her being slammed to the floor. Yodi then allegedly grabbed a hammer from the wooden end table, that was still sitting from her hanging new curtains, then pursued smacking his partner across the face knocking her unconscious with one blow.

A blacked-out Yodi continued striking her in the head with the hook part of the hammer forcing him to yank it out her skull, time after time as he did. Allegedly, Yodi described the blows as similar to taking bites out of a fresh crisp apple . After the savage beating, a still-dazed Yodi, drenched in blood, exited the house walking to the bus stop, where he was noticed and swiftly nabbed by the authorities.

The nigga Yodi cool, but got a head with no screws in it. I don't know what he did or didn't do, nor am I judging, so me and Yodi straight. I just hope whatever he got going on with him can hold off, to at least my visit come this week.

On the day-to-day, I'm rotating with him much more than my guys, but I can trust neither, at this point.

As I simmer in my thoughts, feeling jittery, imagining what I'ma say at my visit tomorrow, out of nowhere Yodi enters the room and screams, "BD!" while smacking my leg hard as hell, startling me. "Barbershop in about an hour, lil nigga. Get ready if you going."

"Damn, Breed, you gonna break my shit," I sigh in numbing pain.

"Get yo' weight up with yo' hate lil nigga. You going or not?"

"No doubt." I hop up, limping, and start preparing.

"Barbershop, barbershop!" the guard yells. Seven guys up and out headed to get fresh cuts. I know I got a visit coming tomorrow night, so crispy my lining out is all I know. When we arrive at the barbershop, it's already packed, but they getting mafuckas in and out with drive-by cuts, straight fucking niggas up.

So I'm patiently just sitting around waiting on my turn and notice one of the guys reckless eye-balling me. He sees me, and I see him, but he doesn't say shit, so you know I'm silent as well. "Next," the barber yells. He hops out of the chair, wipes his forehead, and heads toward the door.

"BD, what deck you on?" he asks me, looking devious as fuck.

"C4. What deck you on?" I rewind his words while mirroring his look. "What's up?"

"I'm on C3. How many BD's up there with you?" he nosily asks.

"Two," I answer. "Why?"

"We need to holla at you, so a mafucker gonna hit you on the vent," he says and walks off. Dam these Vicks really plotting, but I can't go.

After my quick lining, I'm back on the deck chilling, and just as the nigga said, Boom, boom, boom, C4, C4. Send lil Wild hundreds BD to the vent. C4, C4."

One of the GDs taps on my bars: "The vent, Joe." Damn, this Pussy ain't give me enough time to get the hair from behind my fucking ears.

"I ain't trying to hear shit," I mumble as I hop to my feet and walk to the vent. "Boom, boom, C3. This me; what's up?"

"Ay, BD, when you get off the deck, come down here. I gotta holla at you. You going on a visit tomorrow?" he asks.

"Yeah," I reply but shouldn't have told him shit.

"Well, come down here before you go real quick; BD business."

"A'ight, I got you," I say and walk off.

All the rest of the day I'm hawking the vent, making sure they ain't beating on that bitch, directing no BDs towards me. I know some shysty moves going on.cause I'm in this shit, but once again, I ain't going, no matter what it is. Pretty much everything goes smoothly the rest of the evening, but I'm definitely falling to sleep choking my knife.

Clack, clack, clack. Doors popping early, breath-stinking hours. "BD, you eating breakfast?" Yodi asks.

"I'm good on that Akunu today, but grab them milk cartons so we can cook later," I replied. I ain't get much sleep, so I instantly roll back over and im out that quick.

Within two hours or so, *tap tap tap.* What the fuck? The knocks on my bars wake me so fast, I hear my last snore still lingering in the air. "BD, BD. Do you hear that?" *Ping, ping, ping.* "The Latin Kings back there making knives."

Damn, here we go again. Now I'm up on my feet like a fireman, throwing my shit on. "They snatched down the lights and broke both of the mops," he says, huffing and puffing, fumbling his words.

"Calm down, Folks. We gonna holler at Poker and see what's up, because they know they bogus. Come on." Now we on pursuit to find Poker, and I locate him and a few Latin Kings in the back of the hall.. As we begin to get closer, I can hear the sharpening of the knives in one of the King's cells. "Come on now, Poker, what's up with y'all breaking up the mops ? You gotta make them stop."

"BD, you know how this shit goes. We ain't on shit, though.

Y'all get the next set to clean up with," he chuckles, while pulling on his ponytail.

"Poker, niggas on high alert, and y'all know how this shit goes as well. That's why y'all gotta stop."

"We ain't worried about nothing. We ain't worried 'bout shit," his lil King partner blurts out, while flashing a .25 automatic handgun. A chrome beauty, with a pink, shiny handle. A real pocket rocker, that fits right in the palm of your hand. I wish I could take that bitch from him because lil dude is unstable. He doesn't need to be in possession of that.

This lil man talking out the side of his neck, but I ignore him, still staring straight at Poker. "You gotta make them stop," I repeat.

"I got you, I got you," he replies, and me and BD stroll off.

I can't believe they got a fucking gun on the deck. What the fuck is going on in this place? I calm down all the riled-up guys with the news, because none of they ass wanna get popped anyway; I'm sure of that. "The making of the knives stopped for now, so let me go lay my ass back down for a minute.

Only down for about three hours or so, give or take. *Tap tap tap* wakes me, yet fucking again. "BD, the vent," a voice floats through my bars. *Father God, help me,* I think. I'ma kill one of these niggas because I see they ain't gonna stop.

"Boom, boom, C3. This me, what y'all want?" I yell through the vent.

"You still going on that visit today like you said?" he asks.

"Yeah."

"Stop down here before you go." (Silence). "Do you hear me?"

"Yeah, I got you," but I know this nigga out his rabbit-ass mind if they think I'm pulling up on them before my visit.

Silly them. My visit will be here in a few, so me and Yodi just sit around playing casino until it's time. "Dotts, visit," the guard yells. As I retreat to my cell with my heart pumping with anticipation, I flip up my mat and yank my creased visit outfit, then grab my crispy pair of track Nikes, and I'm out.

I'm excited about my little chicken-and-dumplings in the building for me, so I'm feeling good. The communication I've been having with her via money orders, letters, phone calls, etc., is great. One of my GD homeys from the hundreds plugged me with her a few months back, and we still going strong.

"Dotts, booth 2." Okay. As I sit anticipating her presence, I'm shaking like a crap game in the cold. I guess I'm just a lil nervous, to say the least.

Greens, beans, potatoes, tomatoes, chicken, lamb hog, mogs, *you name it.* 'Cause, oh Lord, I tell y'all, when lil baby stepped from around that corner, cheesing, looking like a pretty seasoned pot roast, with potatoes and carrots and shit, I instantly got hungry. Despite Kevin Samuels critiquing at this moment, I wanna eat her up, and the thirst is real. *This is the woman that just might break my pussy-eating virginity,* Im thinking.

"Hey, baby, how you holding up?" She speaks softly. "And may I add, you look so good, my pussy wet."

"Yeah, um, I'm okay, and thanks for the compliment. You

look good as well, baby, but you can't be talking like that. I can't be sitting here with a hard dick in these DOC pants, woman," I whisper. We laugh and enjoy each other until it's over, and just that fast I am back to reality.

Upon me leaving my visit, I remember to stop on C3 to see what these niggas got up they sleeves. I already know what the so-called guys on; I wanna just make sure it's that. I'm addressing everything, but ain't really shit to holla about at this point. Im self governed, so It is what it is.

As soon as I swing the door open, I see one of the so-called guys on the phone. We lock eyes, and he drop his call like the Feds are on his hot-ass boost mobile. At the same time, out the back spring a few more of the BDs, and they all approach the bars with deceitful smiles. "What's up?" I blurt out, with a face that says it all.

"Folks sign up for Muslim service tomorrow, and what happened with that shit over there with the GDs?" he asks.

"Niggas wasn't using they three sixty and got killed because of that shit. That's all I know," I answer.

At the same time amidst our cross-talking, I can hear one of the so called guys try to whisper under his breath to the guard, "Pop the gate." I ain't no damn fool. I know what I heard, so I take off out the door instantly, in mid-convo. These niggas trying to catch me in the stairwell and beat me, kill me, or whatever, I don't know, but I'm gone. I'm not running, but moving at a quick enough pace to stay ahead, hopping two stairs at a time back to my deck.

The sound of multiple rapid, clacking footsteps is all I hear approaching quickly from behind, as I enter my deck. "Pop the gate, pop the gate!" I rush the officer as if I had a bad case of diarrhea. He instantly pops it, but by now they are maybe ten feet behind me, entering the door themselves. *Get there, get there, make it to my knife* is all I'm thinking while power walking to my cell. BDs in pursuit, itching to put their hands on me, storming through the gate, stating, "BD business, BD business," to the onlookers while passing. No sooner than I make it in my cell and reach for my mat, they blitz my room like the Chicago Bears front line.

"Grab him, grab him, put him in the nelson," they insist. Three of the men attempt to do just that, and we fall all over the bed into the bars. The whole time, they trying to grab me and put me in the full nelson, they hitting each other and shit, plus I'm too strong and slippery and definitely going crazy, making it hard for them to keep me down.

Along the struggle, I catch one from a short stiff uppercut to my head and eye. Holding on to slow down some of the damage they inflicting, I got one nigga wrapped by his Fema shielding myself as they punch on my back and the back of my head, like a banjo. These niggas came extra cautious because they actually scared doing what they doing, so it isn't long before they're out of my room feeling accomplished. I instantly hop up because they ain't really do shit; I'm good.

What a mafucking day, I think, staring in the dull mirror at my pain-stricken face, that boomeranged back to me. Damn, all I see is both of my eyes kind of swollen, as I pat them with my fingers. Them beating on my back was also nothing, so I'm good despite a banging headache. Thank God they ain't stab me or shit, so I can live with that. Them dirty dogs knew to pull the stunt when I went on my visit, knowing I wouldn't be strapped. It's all good, 'cause if they like it, I love it, I giggle to myself.

"BD. you good," one of the Moes says exiting his room as well.

"Yeah, I'm good," I reply, rubbing my head.

"I heard you in there Hooting and Hollering. I'm just checking on you, making sure you straight." He chuckled, and we laughed our lil stomachs off together, but ain't shit funny, though. I really need to know who called this bogus violation, considering I know Tory is still down bad. These niggaz than whipped me bogusly, what the fuck they think I don't understand the dynamics of a power shift. I'm my own BD from this point on: if niggas ain't honoring Law, I ain't honoring them, straight like that.

Maybe two weeks or so crawl by, and they call yard early morning. I'm due for some fresh air so I'm up and out, tired and all. Damn, it's bright out here. I barely can see, but this sun feels so good smacking my face while walking my lap solo just imagining about the other side of that wall.

The voices from a crowd of six or seven men twenty feet in front of me knocked me out of my thoughts. They pretty much slow dragging, so I catch up to pass them kind of quickly. As I walk around the crowd not to split them, I see it's the so-called guys, "What's up, BD?" one of the men says, and I just look at them, clenched fist, and keep walking right past they ass, while they talk behind my back. I guess my presence has ruffled their feathers as I walk along, not giving a single solitary fuck. The guards must have caught wind of what their body languages was saying towards me and ended yard shortly after. Somebody gonna *die* in this bitch by these hands of mine, if the good Lord don't send me home soon; I know that much.

This time dry and slowly crawling along like a snail with nothing to look forward to, but a court date per usual, and uplifting words from time to time from our heaven-sent angel, Mother Fonsuela Nork. Mother Nork is pretty much all we have as far as giving us hope that everything will be okay through prayer. Every man good or bad gets their shit in order whenever she comes to visit. We all feel like little children at that moment, taking in her energy as if she was our biological mother. Everyone cherishes everything about her, down to the tray of crispy fried chicken and personal hygiene products we all receive upon her every visit. So thank you, Mother Nork, for the prayers and belief that, no matter what a man has done, it's still good somewhere in him. Mother Nork you're the real MVP, and I'm here to personally thank you and let you know we all *love you dearly.*

Father God, I come to you in the humblest form, asking you to forgive me for my sins past, present, and future. I thank you for the breath in my body, Lord. I thank you for the Akunu that nourishes my body on the daily. I thank you for my health and the health of my family as well.

Father *God*, I ask that you give me and my rappy's the strength to face the judge with our heads held high, in claiming our innocence. Father *God*, you know what they do not, and only you can judge us, *only you, Father*. .

I unbow my head, feeling a lil refreshed already. I need to get back to sleep, but can't. I'm stressed and worried about my future but have faith at the same time that we'll be okay, as we stand before Judge Greg T. Zuria. All these things gumbo in my mind without a soul to confide in but myself, so try to understand my mental state, reader. I've been through a lot, and by this time I've been on the deck with my rappy AZ and my guy Lil Poo for about a month or so.

Quick intel, Lil Poo is a short yellow young nigga that's known for his famous Eazy E curl he rocks as well as his love for money, cars, clothes, and you know the rest. Yeah, he's a player and all that, but don't let that fool you. He's one of the youngest outstanding members for M.O.B. Jack-of-all-trades, but his number one love is the high he gets from a high-stakes gamble. I got love for Poo; that's my brother from another mother, and he never gotta question my loyalty and vice versa. We did BD from the streets to the high school, and now we cellies. No, I'm not happy about the jail part, but you catch my drift: that's my brother.

"BD, what's up, folks? You good?" Lil Poo asks, rolling over out his nod.

"Yeah, I'm good," I reply, sitting straight up. "I just received news earlier that my lil cousin Jody was killed in a car accident, and I'm fucked up about that. Damn, he was like my lil brother, I'm all cried out though, man."

"Sorry to hear that, BD. That's why you've been so quiet, huh?"

"I really don't know, but I'm telling you I feel like a shook-up Pepsi with baking soda in that bitch, just ready to explode."

"Yeah, I feel you, but you gotta hold your head and try to get some rest. You going home tomorrow, and I'm walking you outta this bitch myself."

"Thanks bro," I reply. And back to counting sheep both of us go.

Clack, clack, clack, my door pop. "Dotts, court!" the guard yells. A startled me awakes in good spirits and starts getting my shit together. My heart beating out my chest heavily, as I stand here brushing my chops. "BD, you gone?" Lil Poo awakes and asks.

"Yeah, I'm gone. Folks, I'ma holla at you in a minute."

"Good luck. Y'all going home today," he says, as I exit the room.

XX

Trial

1H3S, The Numbers Game

"First off, if they follow the law and the evidence in this case, we all should be found *not guilty* of first-degree murder and attempt," I jibber on my route to the dayroom. I have no idea why I always pep talk myself on the way to court. It's just something I do unconsciously, like a boxer coming out for his title fight declaring his victory. Yeah, just that serious for me.

"I see you already posted. Are you ready?" I ask.

AZ looks up from fixing his shoes and says, "I been ready from the time we stepped foot in this bitch. Let's do this."

"Dotts, Colton, court!" the guard yells, and we out the door. This is it, the moment we have all been waiting for. Me, AZ, and Big C chose to fight, fight, fight to the end against the system, and ain't no room for second-guessing either.

It's now 1997, and I feel every bit of it, even if it ends today. This three-year journey, possibly to freedom, has been mentally and physically draining for me and AZ, so you know we quiet in our own worlds strolling to court as usual. Big C coming in from the streets, he's been out on bond for about a year and a half, but as I said before, today is that day above all days.

When we enter the courtroom bullpen, we sit around, still quiet, awaiting our street clothes but growing more anxiously nervous by the second. I'm speed-pacing back and forth, forth and back, walking a hole in the ground. Everything needs to go right today, no bullshit, and I hope AZ and his lawyer don't get to clowning either.

"Colton, Dotts, get dressed and do it quickly. Court about to start soon," the guard states. I'm praying Missy dropped off the right stuff, and she did. *Thank you, Sis,* as I grab my basic kit from the guard and transform in no time. Nothing flashy, just something presentable for the judge, but these shiny black shoes and slacks with the white button-down got me ready for war.

Despite our quietness and mindful thinking to ourselves, me and AZ are able to get a small prayer in before we enter the battlefield. ("Our Father, who art in heaven ....") As soon as we enter the courtroom, we're guided to our seats, one high, three straight, hoping for the best, preparing for the worst, challenging the system to war, and yes, we're totally aware of the consequences that gambling with our lives carries. Let's just say this is our cruel reality for the moment and our lives on the line, but ain't no turning back; it's the only way for me.

Now seated, I take a quick glance around and see familiar faces that I haven't seen or heard from until now, as phony as they are. I definitely don't appreciate the fake love they displaying, especially knowing some of them are just in attendance to make sure I ain't getting out this bitch. But listen, reader, we right here. I mean we so close to the door, I can smell it.

Knock, knock from the gavel. "All rise for the Honorable Judge Greg T. Zuria presiding, on court case docket 94-Cr-02299-GZ. In the case of the State versus Gaymon Sparks, Aron Colton, and Appahummie Dotts, on first-degree murder and attempt to cause bodily harm charges."

"The State may proceed, and you can have a seat," the judge says.

"Ladies and gentlemen, we are here today to show motive and insert the truth, about what happened to Mr. Darius Brown. The presented facts and evidence will show you both motive and premeditated murder without a reasonable doubt. It'll also show that Appahummie Dotts, Aron Colton, and Gaymon Sparks killed a man in gang retaliation, so without further ado, Your Honor, the State calls Officer Marcus Turd to the stand."

Who the fuck is this? I'm thinking, as a fully uniformed acornhead-ass CPD officer pops out the back approaching the stand. "Raise your right hand. Do you swear to tell the truth, the whole truth, and nothing but the truth, so help you God?"

"I do," Officer Turd responds.

"You may take a seat and proceed," the judge notes.

The prosecution wastes no time diving right in with the questioning. "Please state your name and occupation."

"Marcus Turd."

"And can you spell it out to the court, please?"

He does. "And I'm employed by the fifth district Chicago police department."

"Mr. Turd, on October/7/1994 do you remember the situation that brings you to court today?"

"Yes."

"Can you please tell us in your words what happened?"

"On that evening I was working the West Pullman area in the fifth district when dispatch alerted that shots were fired around 101st and Cottage Grove."

"And what did you do then?"

"At that time I was three to four miles away, so I hit my overhead lights and sirens and proceeded to the scene. Upon my arrival, I noticed some police activity right outside of the London Towne apartments, so I pursued and turned into the complex. As I'm driving in, I noticed a black four-door box Chevy zipping past me going in the opposite direction towards the exit, so I busted a U-turn and proceeded after the car."

"Were you able to make a stop on the car?"

"Yes."

"Okay, Mr. Turd, as you pursued the fleeing car like you just stated, how many people were present in the car at the time of the stop?"

"Three."

"I have no further questions, Your Honor."

"Would the defense like to cross-examine the witness?" the judge asks.

"Yes, Your Honor," my public defender says while rising

from her seat. *Oh Lord, I know she freaking kidding me, what is she doing?* I'm thinking, watching this lady walk towards the stand. "Mr. Turd, how fast do you think you made it to London Towne apartments after the dispatch alerted shots were fired?"

"Um, maybe five or six minutes, tops."

"So you made it there pretty quickly."

"Yes, I'd say I arrived on the scene pretty quick."

"Okay, Mr. Turd, so what did you observe when you arrived on the scene?"

"As I pulled up I noticed another CPD unit as well as an unmarked cruiser, right outside the exit of the apartments."

"Is that all you saw?"

"No, before I turned into the apartments, I could see what appeared to be the officer of the unmarked car outside his cruiser squatting down, but I kept turning into the apartments. I then drove maybe a hundred feet or so, when I noticed a car speeding going in the opposite direction of me heading towards the exit, so I made a U-turn in pursuit of the fleeing car. I was able to pull it over, in doing so taking all occupants in for questioning."

"Okay, Mr. Turd, do you see any of the men, you took in for questioning that evening in the courtroom today?"

"Yes."

"Can you please point out the defendants you pulled over and took into custody that night?"

"Yes." As Officer Turd straightens his slouched body. he points directly at us and says, "I only see two of them."

"Can you please repeat that, sir?"

"I said, I only see two of them."

My PD instantly gets a jolt of energy from somewhere, and she damn near bites her lip off trying to get her next question out. "Mr. Turd, for the court records which two men are you referring to?"

"Aron Colton and Gaymon Sparks."

"I have no further questions, Your Honor," and she pimped back towards us with a face of stone.

"Thank you, Mr. Turd. You may step down," the judge says.

Damn, I'm thinking to myself, *smart move from my PD, but let's carry on.* The whispers and devilish looks from the prosecution made me feel exactly like they ass, for a slight moment until a wimpy echoed voice blares out, "Ladies and gentlemen, the State calls Ms. Laria Claws to the stand. —You swear to tell the truth, the whole truth, and nothing but the truth, so help you God?"

"I do." As she removes her right hand from the Bible and takes her seat. I'm staring at this girl in disbelief because I've never seen her, nor the CPD officer that just took the stand.

"Ms. Claws, on October/7/1994, do you remember what brings you to court today?"

"Yes."

"Can you please describe to the court what you remember?"

"Yes, I'll never forget that life-changing day for me. I mean, me and Darius were just joyriding around sipping Cisco, kissing our little faces off, that's it. We then wanted to smoke a few joints so Darius suggested we get a nickel bag of weed from London Towne apartments, where he knew a few guys from school. So we rode down 111th street going west to Cottage Grove, then bust a right, turning in the apartments on 103rd Cottage."

"What happened next, Ms. Claws?"

"We pulled in and parked as if he did this before." Her slight pause of silence and rapid breathing let me know it was coming. *Here the fuck we go with the emotions.*

"Take your time, Ms. Claws. Breathe." Memories and emotions flared as she begin to cry on the stand recalling that horrific night, staring in our direction. "What happened next, Ms. Claws?"

"We sat for maybe two or three minutes. Then I noticed two or three people, but only one walking towards us with his hand in his pocket, but I'm thinking nothing of it. I mean, I really thought it was who Darius was waiting on, so I continued fixing my hair in the mirror. Then outta nowhere, loud gunshots go off, (pow, pow). It sounded like they were going off in the car. I didn't know, I didn't know—they were shooting at us until it stopped, and I could see Darius slumped over the steering wheel gasping for air, as well as bleeding from his mouth and nose."

"Ms. Claws, do you see the man in the courtroom today that was approaching the car?"

"Yes, he's sitting in the middle of the three," she whimpered as tears mud slide down her face. Mixed reactions from the onlookers cause cross-whispers to begin. "Quiet," the judge says, and with one blow from the gavel the whispers fade. "State, you may proceed."

"For the record, Your Honor, Ms. Claws has pointed out Aron Colton."

Sickened and angered by the lies, lies, lies, I can hear AZ mumbling angrily under his breath, "This some bullshit," but I never look his way.

"Ms. Claws, did you see anyone else with Mr. Colton as he approached the car?"

"No, but I noticed a silhouette of a body from a short distance before he start shooting."

"The State has no further questions, Your Honor."

"Ms. Claws, you may step down," the judge says.

Shit, that was intense. I'm sweating but feel like I can't even move to wipe it. I'm scared to death as the woman leaves the courtroom, oozing pain and hurt. But what's even more fucked up than that is, to this day I still don't know how the man look who we in jail for. So with that being said, I do understand his family seeking justice, but it's *just not us.* I'm confident taking this bench trial because by law, the judge has to follow law. Personally, I don't need twelve most likely racist mafuckas prejudging over my case and my race, and my rappy's feel the same. I'd rather stay with the man who looked me in my face for the whole three years.

"Mr. Dotts, it's looking good. Like I said before, you were never pointed out at any time," the PD whispers while clutching my knee. Those words knock me out of my daze, sending me on a high as if we have already beaten this case.

"Is Jarvus Powers here?" I asked.

"Yes, he's here," she whispered, and just that fast, those high emotions fell to the floor once again. How could this dirty bastard be here doing this to us? I thought we were BDs; I thought we were partners. Damn, how did it come to this? I guess he feels the law's grip on his bitch ass is way more sinister than what we can offer. I wish I could call him a snitch, but I can't. There are no words that can possibly describe a person who'll do anything to save his own ass, who wasn't even in trouble. A damn shame you so frightened of jail and the police that you'd conspire a whole make-believe story with them to take innocent lives away from their families so you could get let the fuck go. (Now, reader, what name y'all got for him? I'll wait!) The closest name I could call him would be a *rat*, but that's still not potent enough.)

Without further ado, ladies and gentlemen of the court, "The State calls Jarvus Powers to the stand." Oh shit, shit then got real. This nigga really here to testify against us, knowing we ain't do shit, but here we go. Out the back walks Jarvus, and my heart dropped to my toes. I ain't seen this clown face in three years, not to mention he got the same exact scared-ass look he had at 111th police station after they grabbed us. "Raise your right hand. Do you swear to tell the truth, the whole truth, and nothing but the truth, so help you God?" He responds yes, and the State proceeds. "Can you please state your name for the court?"

"Jarvus Powers."

"Can you please spell it out?" He does so. "Mr. Jarvus Powers, on October 7, 1994, do you remember who you were with and how you ended up in London Towne apartments in the West Pullman area in Chicago, Illinois?"

"Yes, I was riding with Gaymon Sparks, Aron Colton, and Appahummie Dotts."

"Do you see any of those gentlemen in this courtroom today, Mr. Powers?"

"Yes," he replies.

"For the record, can you point the three gentlemen out in the courtroom?" With no hesitation a fake stand up nigga, now he sit down and aim us out one by one. Then the questioning begins.

"Mr. Powers, isn't it a fact that you stated to Chicago homicide Detective Jody Brinks and officer Lester Conard that you and two other defendants were harassed in a parked car in London Towne apartments, by three men throwing up gang signs and brandishing weapons, isn't that correct?"

"Yes," he answers.

"You also stated that gang signs and quotes were directed toward you, as well as the other two defendants, right?"

"Yes," he replies.

"Isn't it a fact they asked what gang you guys were in, and you stated you were BDs, but your friend, who was the driver, he's a Vice Lord?"

"Yes."

"You also stated that the driver of the car, who is known

as Gaymon Sparks, was in the house when the three men approached the car, is that correct?"

"Yes."

"Isn't it also a fact you stated they threatened to put a hole in your head first if they didn't see a Vice Lord driving the car on the way out?"

"Yes."

"Mr. Powers, did you and the defendants leave the London Towne apartments without further altercations?"

"Yes," he replies again. I'm sitting here, palms sweating, and my legs shaking like a leaf on a tree, but I'm content.

"Isn't it true that Mr. Sparks exited the house and drove you and the two defendants back to the Gardens Public Housing projects and retrieved a loaded .380 handgun after receiving the news of what had just happened?" "Yes."

"I object, Your Honor," Big C's lawyer stands and states.

"On what ground?" the judge asks.

"That the State is painting a negative picture of my client by stating the housing projects as his location."

"Overruled, says the judge. "Counsel for the State, you may proceed."

"Mr. Powers, isn't it a fact you stated that your cousin got out of the car, and was replaced by Aron Colton for the return trip to London Towne apartments?"

"Yes."

"Isn't it a fact that you and the three defendants returned to the same London Towne apartments brandishing a loaded .380 handgun, shortly after?"

"Yes."

"Mr. Powers, who in fact had possession of the .380 handgun upon returning to London Towne homes?"

"Appahummie Dotts," he states in a low, whimpered voice.

"Mr. Powers, isn't it a fact that Mr. Dotts handed the gun off to Mr. Colton before they exited the car?"

"No."

Jarvus's response really startles the prosecution as well as everyone else, but with a look of shock on her face, she moves on.

"Isn't it also a fact that the three defendants hopped out of the car when they spotted one of the men who approached you guys just earlier, now sitting parked?"

"No," Jarvus replies.) Immediately the oohs and whispers flood the courtroom from the spectators once again. This could be good for us, his punk ass having a change of heart or something, because he telling the truth. *Knock, knock* as the judge's gavel bangs order back in his courtroom. The anxious onlookers settle from the judge's command, and the State proceeds.

"Mr. Powers, calm down. You're okay, you're fine. Nothing is going to happen to you. Take a deep breath, have a drink of water, and let's proceed. Remember: you have nothing to worry about." I guess her devilish tone comforted his scared evil soul.

"Let's try this again, Mr. Powers. Isn't it a fact that the three defendants hopped out of the car, Mr. Colton now brandishing the gun that Mr. Dotts handed him, to seek revenge on one of the men that approached you guys throwing up gang slogans just earlier?"

"Yes."

"And in doing so, Mr. Colton fired off five shots in retaliation through the driver's window, killing Darius Brown, while Mr. Dotts and Sparks stood positioned as the lookouts?"

"Yes," he replies, sitting straight up like the King of the South. *You gotta be kidding me,* I think as the onlookers take back off into emotional chatters.

Bang, bang, the wooden gavel slams again. "Order," *bang,* "order," as the crowd silences. "If we have any more interruptions from anyone, you will be charged with contempt of court and will be taken into custody immediately. Does the State have further questions?"

"Yes, Your Honor."

"Then you may proceed."

"Isn't it also a fact that you stated all three defendants ran back to the car where you noticed Mr. Colton pass Mr. Dotts the .380 handgun?"

"Yes, I was just waking up."

"Isn't it also a true statement that Mr. Dotts jumped out of the speeding car with the gun while being pursued by CPD fleeing London Towne apartments?"

"Yes."

"No further questions, Your Honor."

"You may step down Mr. Powers." This goat-mouth bitch, Jarvus exited the stand as instructed while the whole courtroom stared at his slouched body in silence being escorted to the back. I'm sitting here looking at this clown in disbelief. I can't believe this nigga just did this shit. He really trying to get us hung in this bitch.

"Does the State have any more witnesses?"

"No, Your Honor," the State replies.

"Does the defense have any witnesses or any other questions?" "No, Your Honor," each of our separate counsel answers the judge's request.

I can't believe this shit. This crooked ass prosecutor lady repeated the same questions as before, but now Jarvus rotten-ass lying on us.

I know this nigga is confusing people I'm sure, but the only true statement was I did hop out of a speeding car with a pistol that I had the whole time. AZ never gave me anything. (*"But we still ain't kill nobody or know nothing about it."*) And peep this, the tricky part about it is, the law never saw me hop out of the car, so they never knew I was in the car, to begin with until someone informed them.

Reader, Jarvus Powers knows what happened. He was there, but now he laying across the judge's desk with flowers in his mouth, Ole bitch made, Gump, chump ass nigga, fuck you, acting as a victim in a coerced murder trial, against his so-called friends. The lil nigga wasn't raised right by his pussy big brother if you ask me. I kid you not, my mind, body, and soul froze in la-la land, and the only thing I can feel right now is my eight fingers and two thumbs wrapping his motherfucking neck.

"Mr. Dotts, Mr. Dotts." My PD startles and unfreezes me again. "Sit up, sit up. The judge is about to read the verdict, and may God bless you." You think I was scared before, her "may God bless you" words petrified me because they only assured me of how much trouble I was in and how much I needed him to take the wheel and guide us through this verdict.

All rise as the judge prepares to read the verdicts. This is the first time I glanced at my rappy's all trail, and from what I can see, we all got noodle legs and scared shitless.

The judge: "Ladies and gentlemen, in the court case docket 94-Cr-02299-GZ, the State versus Gaymon Sparks, Aron Colton, and Appahummie Dotts. Court ruling on first-degree murder and attempt to cause bodily harm, I find the defendant Gaymon Sparks *not guilty* of all charges."

As the crowd roars in cheers and pouts, all I feel is the whole table move. That not guilty verdict chopped Big C big ass down like a tree.

"In court case docket 94-Cr-02299-GZ, the State versus Aron Colton, I find the defendant *guilty* of first-degree murder, and *not guilty* of the attempt to cause bodily harm."

"Aww, hell naw!" AZ screams in pain and disbelief and damn near flips the table over as well, sending the whole courtroom in an uproar yet again. His painful sobbing cries and screams of "We ain't do shit. Fuck all you bitches!" repeat his vocab for the judge and everyone else to witness. As the guard approaches, I'm shook up and barely standing myself, watching the hurt and pain AZ is feeling right now, despite my own fate not being read yet.

"In court case docket 94-Cr-02299-GZ, the State versus Appahummie Dotts on first-degree murder and attempt to cause bodily harm, I find the defendant *not guilty* of first-degree murder and attempt to cause bodily harm, but find the defendant *guilty* of possession of a firearm."

"What he say?" "What he say?" as loud chatter from the onlookers shot to the roof again. I know I heard a *not* in there somewhere.

"Congratulations, congratulations, Mr. Dotts. You're going home to your family. Congratulations." My two PDs joyfully celebrate me with pats and squeezes on my shoulders, but I'm numb to reality at this moment. Boy oh boy, no roller coaster ride in the world feels like this one. I'm happy as hell and can't believe I'm going home to my family, but on the other hand, sad as hell and can't believe AZ staying here with all the alleged killers.

"Counsel, how's the twenty-fifth of May looking on your calendars?"

"Our day is open, Judge."

"Defense, does May twenty-fifth work for you guys as well?"

"Yes, Your Honor, it does."

"For the record, on May twenty-fifth at ten a.m. the sentencing of Aron Colton on first-degree murder charges. Also, the sentencing of Appahummie Dotts on misdemeanor possession of a firearm charge." Bang from the gavel. "This court is adjourned," and the judge spins around in his seat, disappearing like magic.

At this very moment, our fate has been sealed, and I'm not knowing how to feel as they guide us back to the bullpens, this shit got my mind speed-balling. During the brief walk, AZ's lawyer tries to soothe him with appeal talk, but he not trying to hear shit at all, and I don't blame him. It's really like we all lost the fight because my victory is a bittersweet one.

Bittersweet is definitely what it is, because AZ going crazy, and I gotta sit here and compose my true feelings about my own victory in regaining my freedom back. I'm mentally drained and can't comprehend how he feeling right now, so I bowed my head in my lap, and me and Granddad pray for AZ's mental state.

Moreover, the route back to Division 1 is a long, quiet walk. *Conceal your thoughts, Appahummie,* I keep telling myself. I can't even properly look AZ in his face and say everything gonna be ok, because I'd be lying. It's nothing you can say to a falsely accused innocent man who's lost his life behind bogus allegations. That's right, you can't say shit, so I keep my mouth shut, keep walking, and rejoice in my win, on the inside.

Cries, Smiles, and Cries

The jiggling of keys shakes my mind back to reality and lets me know we've arrived back to the C Whale. As soon as the door opens and the gate pops, all I can see are puzzled staring faces, from all mobs in attendance. *Here the fuck we go with the twenty-one questions*, I'm knowing. I can see it all in these niggas' faces. Somebody ready to blurt some silly shit out their mouth and fuck around and kick the deck off.

"What happened? How y'all get found not guilty, but he did? Did he have a paid lawyer? What y'all took, a bench or a jury?" Blah, blah, fucking blah. However, AZ strolls past all their asses, straight to his room, with a look on his face that says, *It's over. Now we can play.* I bop past the dayroom, mirroring AZ as well.

Lil Poo the first nigga waiting in the hallway as AZ breezes by him with me following. "What happened?" Li'l Poo says, looking as nervous as me.

"Me and Big C beat it, and AZ lost, but they found me guilty of possession of a firearm. I gotta go for sentencing on the twenty-fifth of next month."

"Hell yeah, hell yeah," Li'l Poo states, excited as we embrace with pure joy. "What about AZ?" he asks.

"I don't know, bro. Shit all bad."

"Damn, AZ," Li'l Poo mumbles to himself.

Those two words brew an overflowing pot of pain, hurt, and emotions that pour out my soul into tears that trickle onto his shoulder. "Li'l Poo, I love you, BD. I don't wanna leave you in here with these niggas, bro. What you gon' do? You gotta promise me you gon' make it out this bitch."

"I'm good, I'm good. I love you too, bro, but you going

home to your family. Let's just worry about that right now," he scolds me. "You got another shot at life; don't fuck it up."

"I won't, I won't. I got you, bro. Well, I'm tired as hell. I'm about to go lay it down. What a fucking day."

"Yeah, get you some rest, BD."

"A'ight.

"*Guilty.* Mr. Dotts, you have been found guilty of first-degree murder by a jury of your peers and sentenced to *life.* Ha-ha-ha-ha-ha!"

"Noooooooo!" I scream. The judge's devilish laugh leaves me falling from a darkened sky, in a claustrophobic panic.

"Wake up, wake up!" Li'l Poo is shaking me. "Wake up!"

"Ahhhh, you scared the shit outta me, Poo. Damn."

"Naw, nigga, your nightmares did that to you. You been screaming in your sleep all week."

"Well, you're a day late and a dollar short, because you should've been woke me up, in that case."

We both just lie there laughing, but in reality, that nightmare still on my mind, heavy. As the days get closer and closer to our sentencing, AZ still ain't mumbled a word, straight zombied out. Over my time here, I've heard many men cursing the man up above about their situations and how it played out for them. I often wonder, if my outcome was different, would I be one of the same? Who knows, but this shit is deep, and it gets deeper for some. So advice to you, reader: no matter young, old, blind, cripple or crazy, please, I repeat, please, stay out them people's way, because they already hunting us from hell, and you don't want none of this life. Trust me.

Sentencing
Bitter Sweet

May 25, 1997. Thank you, thank you, thank you, Father. The day has finally arrived, and I bullshit you not, this thirty days to sentencing felt just about longer than the whole entire time I been in here altogether. Me and Li'l Poo are already up lurking when our door pops; we ain't been to sleep.

"Dotts, Colton, court." Damn, I feel high as fuck right now, and I can't explain it. But one thing I could explain is why AZ ain't in the dayroom yet ready to go. I'm sure y'all know as well, but when he appears, we gone. Our route to court is the same as always, drama, chaos, and banging all around, but not an uttered word from either of us.

When we arrive to court, the bullpen is bone dry and empty, so it looks like it's me and AZ all alone. Keep in mind, I'm going home today, and AZ getting sentenced for a first-degree murder, and these judges passing out football numbers.

Click, clack as they release these tight-ass cuffs and place us in the bullpen. And just that quick, before I can even rub my wrists good, AZ lawyer at the bars with that appeal talk again, and AZ not hearing that shit at all. We sit for a dry fifteen or twenty minutes, which feels like fifteen or twenty hours.

"Dotts, Colton, let's go."

"Hold on, hold on, guard. I thought we go in separate," I say.

"No, you go together. Who told you that?"

"I just thought," I mumble with an extra-large heartbeat in my chest.

"Let's go." We follow the guard into a freezing cold courtroom and take our seats. I'm sitting here scared as shit, questioning my mind, as if I ain't going home today.

"All rise for the Honorable Greg T. Zuria, presiding." On my feet I am, and AZ ain't bip or bop, and I ain't mad at him for shit.

After several taps from his attorney, AZ rises to face his fate, from someone who will be judged himself one day.

Knock, knock from the gavel. "Ladies and gentlemen, on court case docket, 94-Cr-02299-GZ the State versus Aron Colton on first-degree murder charges. Does the State have anything to say?" the judge asks.

"Yes, we the State ask for the maximum sentence the case carries, Your Honor."

"Mr. Colton, do you have anything to say to the court?"

"Y'all know we ain't do this shit. Fuck all y'all, racist bitches," he says as tears of pain roll down his face.

"Calm down, calm down." His attorney tries to soothe him.

Knock, knock from the gavel. "Mr. Colton, I"—*knock, knock*—"Mr. Colton I've studied this case thoroughly over the course of three years and followed the law by all means."

"No, you didn't," AZ blurts out yet again.

Knock, knock from the gavel. "Mr. Colton, I found you guilty based on the facts and evidence as well as eyewitness testimony in this case. You took a man's life, in doing so taking him away from his family forever, so I will take you away from yours, forever as well. I hereby sentence you to fifty years in the state penal system."

I must have passed out for AZ myself, because when I regain my consciousness, all I hear is an earful of sobs and "Fuck all y'all racist bitches. Y'all know we ain't do this shit. Fuck y'all!" As a slight tussle calms down, AZ looks defeated, being escorted out by the guards. My heart pounding, and I'm shaking for AZ. They gave this man fifty years in my face like that. I'm super scared right about now, I can't lie, as if I'm receiving the same fate or worse. I just want out of this courtroom and out of this place, I swear.

"On court case docket 94-Cr-02299-GZ, the State versus Appahummie Dotts, on misdemeanor possession of a firearm. The court sentences Mr. Dotts to 365 days, time considered served. You're free to go home, sir."

With mixed emotions, I never thank the judge, as I walk off and exit the courtroom, although I am thankful. This shit ain't right; all of us supposed to went home. Signed, sealed, and delivered, I'm out this bitch, and I'm ecstatic to myself, but depressed as well.

As I'm walking up to the bullpen, I can see AZ pacing a hundred miles an hour in circles. I know, I can't console him and definitely don't know what he thinking right now, but I'm on point. I'm not trying to say AZ on something with me; I'm just merely speaking facts because shit like this be fucking niggas' heads straight up.

"What happen?" AZ says, surprising the shit outta me that he opened his mouth to say anything, because he ain't said a word in a month.

"They gave me time considered served," I answered.

"That's what's up, that's what's up," he repeated.

"AZ, man, I'm sorry. Them people know they bogus."

"It's cool, it's cool, but fifty years," he growls. "Fifty motherfucking years. Somebody gon' die in this bitch every day. Old racist bitches, all y'all bitches gon' die soon anyway," he screams as his chest heaves with pain and anger from a frozen black cracked heart.

"Colton, Dotts." The guards approach the bars to cuff us. I can't believe this is my final ride back to Division 1. The long walk back was the same; silence nothing different. When we make it back to the deck, the guys instantly start celebrating my going home. I know they actions have to make AZ sick to his stomach. Not saying he hating or anything; it's just fucked up how this played out and he caught the bad end of the stick.

"Ayye, pipe that shit down," Lil Poo tells the guys and sends everyone away. Boy, I tell you, I love my nigga Lil Poo because he's on top of it. This nigga ain't letting no oppositions or barely the folks get close to me, no matter what. "Didn't I tell you I was walking you out this bitch myself?"

"Hell, yeah, you said it, but I still won't believe it till I see it."

"Dotts, pack it up," the guards yell. Those words seem surreal and alert AZ that I am heading out. I'm not taking shit, so I'm empty-handed as me and Lil Poo approach AZ, while a deck full of men tune in like they watching their favorite soap opera or some shit.

At this moment me and AZ embrace for the last time. "Go fuck some of them hos and tricks for me, and stay outta trouble," he says, voice breaking.

"Yeah, man, I will, and you hold your head up as well."

My homey Lil Poo looks like a puppy dog as he walks me to the bars for the last time. "I love you, Folks. Be safe out there," he says.

"I love you too. You be safe in here."

The guard pops the gate, and I'm Audi 5000.

Being processed out sure doesn't feel like being processed in, I can tell you that much. "Dotts, you're a free man. Enjoy life and make the best of it," the releasing officer states.

"I will," and when they open that door and the sunlight swarms my body, oh what a feeling, Toyota. I'm standing in front of the building looking around in total amazement at the people and all the action going on while waiting for Missy to pull up.

"Hey baby, have you been in there for a long time?" a nice older lady asks me.

I pause and then answer, "Yes, ma'am," still looking amazed.

"I can tell, but God bless you, baby, and welcome back" are her last words before she disappears into the crowd of people.

Welcome back—yeah, I like how that sound, if I do say so myself. *Welcome back to me*, I giggle as I walk off into my future, trusting that I'm still on my way to being the best person and version of me that I can be. "Welcome back."

THE END ...

Sincerely, thanks for the support from all my readers. This story is not to promote gang violence in any shape, form, or fashion. It's merely to create awareness of gang culture, and the severity that lies within a one-sided system where railroading is alive. This story also shows the cruel reality, where a split-second bad decision can land you in a lifelong pot of hot water. So, to my readers, with all due respect, everyone has a past and a story and I'm simply just telling mine. If I can reach one, I can teach one.

Book Blurb

Enter at your own risk, into the dark side of a self-proclaimed hell.

The year is 1994 with record-high murders within the city of Chicago, but this is an in-depth look from the inside of the murderous Cook County Jail Division 1. This is a tale of a blazing fire pit of hell where survival is key and the stakes couldn't be higher in the notorious gang and drug world of the GDs, BDs, Vice Lords, Blackstones, corrupt guards, and a host of others Mobs all feasting under one roof where power and principle propel these gangs into hand-to-hand combat to near-death experiences and beyond.

Nothing or no one could've prepared eighteen-year- old Appahummie Dotts for what he was about to experience as an inmate, navigating through a building full of men accused of every horrific crime imaginable while facing murder charges himself. His guilt or innocence is irrelevant if he wants to stay breathing through all the chaos and violence headed his way, because when it's beef and bad blood in the air, no guards can save you behind these Cook County Jail Division 1 bars, leaving you only two options: you either ride or die. Most say they would ride, but who would've known it would all end like this?

About the Author

officialappahummietheauthor@outlook.com

Appahummie Dotts was only eighteen years old when he entered prison, and nothing prepared him for what he was about to experience as an inmate. This is his story.

IN THE CIRCUIT COURT OF COOK COUNTY, ILLINOIS

THE PEOPLE OF THE STATE OF ILLINOIS
vs.

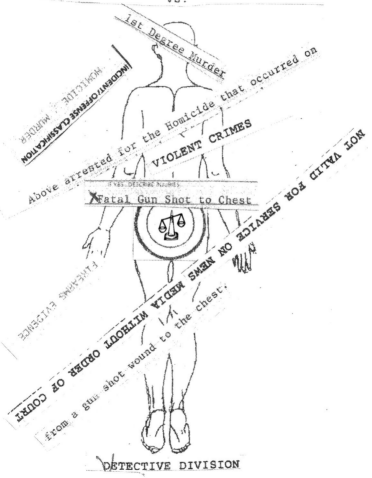

1st Degree Murder

HOMICIDE : MURDER

INCIDENT/OFFENSE CLASSIFICATION

Above arrested for the Homicide that occurred on

VIOLENT CRIMES

NOT VALID FOR SERVICE ON NEWS MEDIA WITHOUT ORDER OF COURT

IF YES, DESCRIBE INJURIES

X Fatal Gun Shot to Chest

FIREARMS EVIDENCE

from a gun shot wound to the chest.

DETECTIVE DIVISION

Printed in the United States
by Baker & Taylor Publisher Services